3.15.78

Papers delivered at the 25th anniversary of the Faculty of Economics of the University of Groningen, the Netherlands.

25 YEARS OF ECONOMIC THEORY

Retrospect and prospect

Edited by

T.J. Kastelein, S.K. Kuipers,
W.A. Nijenhuis, G.R. Wagenaar

Martinus Nijhoff Social Sciences Division
Leiden 1976

ISBN 90 207 0637 3

Preface

Almost three years passed since the Faculty of Economics of the University of Groningen celebrated its 25th Anniversary in 1973. Late, but not too late we hope, to present the lectures of most of our distinguished guests, who came from the United States and different European Countries to inform the Congress participants of their opinion and ideas on "25 Years of Economic Theory: Retrospect and Prospect."

The problems we met in publishing the lectures, in accordance with the agreement we made with our guests, are not unusual, as everyone knows who has been an editor of such a volume before. The promise to give a lecture and to write it down afterwards as well is much more difficult to maintain than only to give a speech. Everybody knows there is nothing so terrifying as to be reminded of your promise to write down your lecture, especially if only a type-written text, put down from a tape, is at your disposal. You are sure of your remembrance: "That very day I heard applause, there were friendly words and perhaps a state of not ending enthusiasm. And now I receive this type-written text of my speech with a request, full of innocence, of these friendly committee members, "will you be so kind as to prepare your text for publication?" But this one, is this my text? Unbelievable. Broken sentences, dots and comma's on the wrong places, half and sometimes badly considered thoughts and sideways." Not all our lecturers had these experiences: some of them have given their written speeches immediately after they lectured, others after some weeks. Some, however, gave them not before a rather long time had passed. Unfortunately, one was not able to prepare his text at all. However, the delay of the date of publication is not only due to the difficulties in preparing the manuscripts. It is also the result of the financial and technical problems that had to be solved in order to make publication possible at all. But now, almost three years after the anniversary, the book is completed. In the outlay of this book we have made two sections. The first one consists of the papers in the field of economics, the second one of those in the field of business economics. At the end of both sections a comment is added.

The papers refer to quite different subjects. From this point of view the collection is rather heterogeneous. However, all papers· are related to each other by one unifying principle: how did the different subjects develop in the past and how will they develop in future? For this reason, it may be worthwhile not only for the congress participants but also for other people interested in economics to read this collection.

T.J. Kastelein
S.K. Kuipers
W.A. Nijenhuis
G.R. Wagenaar

Contents

List of contributors

A.P. BARTEN, Professor of Economics, Centre for Operational Research and Econometrics, Heverlee, Belgium.

A. BOSMAN, Professor of Business Economics, University of Groningen, the Netherlands.

C.W. CHURCHMAN, Professor of Management Science, Schools of Business Administration, University of California, Berkeley, United States of America.

E. JOHNSEN, Professor of Business Administration, The Copenhagen School of Economics and Business Administration, Denmark.

F.J. DE JONG, Professor of Economics, University of Groningen, the Netherlands.

J. PEN, Professor of Economics, University of Groningen, the Netherlands.

H.A. SIMON, Professor of Computer Science and Psychology, Carnegie-Mellon University, Department of Psychology, Pittsburg, Pennsylvania, United States of America.

B. SÖDERSTEN, Professor of Economics, University of Göteberg, Sweden.

G. WILLS, Professor of Marketing and Logistics Studies, Cranfield School of Management, England.

Opening speech

W.F. Duisenberg*

This month it is nineteen years ago that for the first time I entered the buildings of the Faculty of Economics at the State University of Groningen. Much has happened to this Faculty since then, much has happened to me, most perhaps has happened to economics and that is what you are all here for.

Before going into that a little further, I ask your permission to say a few words on another subject. Coming back to one's Alma Mater, on an occasion like this, does not fail to also have an emotional impact. It is with feelings of sorrow and respect that most of us these days will think of those who are not with us any more: Professor Winsemius, Mr. Brinkman, who guided so many of us into the difficult areas of mathematics, and those whom I regard as very personal friends: Professor Jaap Meij, Rieks Willems and Rieks Werkema. May this conference also be regarded as a tribute to them.

You are all here for a few days of reflection on what has happened in the past twenty-five years in the field of economic theory and perhaps on what will happen in the future. I shall not dwell on those subjects. Colleagues much better qualified than I am, are already gathered in this room to shed their light on this.

Almost a year ago, I had a discussion with one of my colleagues at the University of Amsterdam. He said to me that he was getting bored with economics, the reason being his feeling we already knew so much. Nothing new could be produced anymore. The main task of economists and econometricians, so he said, was to perhaps add a second decimal behind the comma of our sophisticated equations. I asked him, if it were true that we already know everything to be known about economic theory, what, if that was true, seemed to be the reason that in practice everything does not seem to go just as theory would suggest. His answer

* Minister of Public Finance.

was very simple: "The politicians". Well, Ladies and Gentlemen, you now see clearly the challenge *I* am confronted with.

But let me quickly add that I have no illusion about the difference it will make for the outcome when in practical policy people who have dwelt considerable time on economic theory have a chance to participate in the decision making process. Problems are too complex, circumstances vary too widely, interests differ too much to lead to the simple solutions that straightforward economic thinking would suggest. In my first year here we used a stencil on mathematics for economists written by prof. Frits de Jong. I clearly remember that in a footnote it said, and it was a quote: "wass die Mathematik allein bewirkt ist ein genaues Denken über ungenaue Dingen." Stretching and abusing that statement a little, one may perhaps say that the only thing economics can do is to promote clear thinking on certain aspects, but by no means all, of a very complex subject-matter. A subject-matter that, when interpreted as the empirical subject of economic theory, continually changes its appearance, hardly ever remaining unchanged long enough to be studied satisfactorily or to be fully understood.

Ladies and Gentlemen, in my opinion there is no reason at all to be bored with economics, because no one ever needs to fear that he will fully understand what is going on in economic life. We shall never be ready.

In a foreword to his excellent textbook on *Macro-economic theory and policy* William Branson explains the set-up of his book. I used it in my course in Amsterdam. In that book he endeavours to provide a mixture of sophisticated economic theories and applied economics, most examples of course being inspired by the American economy. In that way he tries to provide a fair picture of the state of various economic theories and their operational meaningfulness, which as you all of course know, in the mind of at least one prominent economist is the appropriate test for economic theory.

Towards the end of the book, Branson provides quite a few chapters on the theory of economic growth and he states that, although he does present the theory, he cannot yet give the examples and analyses inspired by actual practice of life because the theory of economic growth has not yet reached the stage of operationality. That stage, in his view, is most likely to be reached only in the next decade or so.

Now here is an example of a set of economic theories not yet having become operational and even then the nature of the subject-matter already seems to change. Economic growth itself has become a hot subject of debate in recent years. Now many academicians will of course maintain that the different emphasis on economic growth as such will not and should not have an impact on the theory of economic growth. On the contrary, they would argue that the theory of growth, as developed in the last twenty-five years will only help to better understand the process of economic growth and the ways to manipulate it. I must confess that I am not quite so sure of the immunity of theory to changes in norms and valuations and starting points from which theory derives.

I used this as an example of a set of theories on a subject-matter that has not even become operational before already the subject-matter itself seems to change. But also in the field of short-term economic theory and policy there is no reason to be bored. Let us take a brief look at the economic situation in this country today. There seem to be two overriding short-term problems: a whopping degree of inflation and a level of unemployment which, judged on the basis of our performance in the past decade, must be qualified as too high. Phillips curve where are you?

But then: are they short-term problems; are they just cyclical? For both the answer seems to be: "No, it is not only that."

Inflation, to take the first, has been with us for so long that already for that reason one might be inclined to call it "structural." But then of course the duration of an inflationary process cannot be the adequate criterion for a phenomenon being structural or cyclical. One has to take a closer look. One of the first questions the economist asks, is: "What is it, demand-inflation or cost-push?" Judging from most indices, such as the state of the labour market, the position of the balance of payments, it is not a demand-inflation, so, the economist concludes, "it must be cost-push." Does that mean we have the answer, let alone the solution? I think not.

"Cost-push" is one of those empty or almost-empty boxes of economic theory, that do not help us much in policy-making. Before we can fight inflation successfully, we must know more of the actual processes behind the cost-push phenomenon. One thing policy-makers have become convinced of is that cost-push has a lot to do with the self-reinforcing elements in the inflationary process. Once started, whether from the demand side or by a successful bid for higher incomes in excess of rises in productivity, inflation feeds on itself. Indexation, whether explicit or in fact, transmits any upward movement in prices throughout the economy. Inflation in turn generates inflationary expectations and hence leads to demands that go even further than pure and simple indexation would justify. It is this complex, if you wish "structural", process of self-sustained and self-reinforcing inflation that we must try to break. This is no easy task, one that is certainly much more difficult than the usual Keynesian remedies of demand-management. Here, as elsewhere, economic policy is forced to disaggregate, to look at the different components of the economic process in order to find the appropriate policy for each, where macro-policies have failed.

Like inflation, our present unemployment problem is not purely cyclical either. Certainly, there are elements of cyclical unemployment in it. There are signs, however, of increasing maladjustment between capacity changes as indicated by capital investment and the supply of labour. I only need to mention the increasing duration of the average period of unemployment and the fact that unemployment and the number of vacancies do not seem to show their normal, consistent pattern. The problem becomes even more clear, but also more complex from a point of view of finding the appropriate solution, when one goes into the regional and sectoral breakdown. New areas have to be added to the list of problem-areas of this country, new branches of activity which in the past we have never had any problems of employment with, now cause particular concern to policy-makers in The Hague.

I only touched in a very generalizing way upon a few of the aspects of the two major problems we at present are confronted with: inflation and unemployment. Yet, however generalizing my approach may seem, it is clear that the policy problems are highly complicated and that simple solutions are out of the question. Matters are even more complicated because inflation and unemployment are in a way interrelated, be it not in the way suggested by the familiar Phillips-curve analysis; the structural and accelerating degree of inflation is probably at least one cause of increasing structural unemployment. If this is correct, and I believe it is, an attack on the inflationary process in itself may contribute to the solution of the problem of the structurally high unemployment level.

Now from the nature of the present inflationary process, it is not only quite clear that in the long run nobody gains from inflation, but it also can be maintained that no real loss is involved when an attack on inflation is waged; on the contrary, if it is true that inflation itself is one cause of increasing unemployment in the present set-up, then a reduction of the inflationary spiral will only be beneficial for unemployment, particularly in the longer run. This seems to be an ideal starting-point for a process of consultations with all parties suffering from, involved in and bearing responsibility for the process of inflation and unemployment, that is to say the Government, the employers and the unions. If the latter two categories can be convinced, as we are, that fighting the present type of inflation will not require *real* sacrifices but only *nominal* sacrifices, it would seem that we stand a good chance of indeed doing something about these two ugly problems.

Next week, the Government will present its program with which it hopes to set the stage for a round of consultations with the social partners in order to acquire their cooperation for the economic policy to be pursued. It is in the interest of all that these consultations will succeed.

This, Ladies and Gentlemen, concludes what I wanted to say to you today; it will, unlike Peyton Place, be continued exactly one week from now.

Mr. Chairman, Ladies and Gentlemen, I wish you a very good conference which I now declare opened. Thank you.

PART I

Trends in the analysis of consumer demand*

A.P. Barten

1. Introduction

"The nearer an epoch is to us, the less we understand it: our own we understand least of all." It is fitting to start with this disclaimer quoted from the monumental *History of Economic Analysis* by Schumpeter. Indeed, when discussing present developments, one has not the benefit of hindsight while it is also virtually impossible to obtain an overview over what all is going on in our economic discipline, even not in that relatively neat area of the theory of consumer demand. To evaluate possible trends is a task notoriously full of pitfalls and undoubtedly the present attempt will be no exception.

Consumption is the *raison d'être* of the economic process. We do not consume to produce but we produce to consume. Consumption is also associated with well-being, the quality of life. To have a close look at · how economists approach consumption in their theories seems to be an inevitable part of the stock-taking of the present state of economic theory. Moreover, the present feelings of crisis express themselves frequently in a criticism on our actual patterns of consumption. The prophets of doom predict that we are consuming ourselves to death in a not too distant future. The euphoria of the late fifties and early sixties, when some talked about a new golden age, has ended in a loud protest against our refrigerator society. The negative external effects of a number of popular consumer goods have never been before so obvious as nowadays. The lack of adjustment of publicly provided consumer goods

---

* This text was prepared for oral presentation. For reasons of oratorical smoothness no references to sources have been made. An apology is due to all persons to whom this does not justice. Many persons active in demand analysis might find that their ideas and approaches are not adequately treated, for which I also apologize. The format of a lecture has confined me to a discussion of a limited choice of topics. The fact that some topics were included and others left out should not be interpreted as a reflection of their relative importance.

and services complementary to private ones is another cause for unhappiness with the present state of affairs. While in the Northern hemisphere people were never materially so well off as now, millions elsewhere on the world are falling below the level of physical subsistence. For some our consumption patterns tend to dehumanize rather than to develop mankind away from a materialistic existence.

Of course, this feeling of unhappiness about our present consumption patterns is only a part of the crisis syndrome of our days. In our Western societies, that profess to be essentially egalitarian, the existence of almost unassailable pockets of power or, otherwise said, the unequal distribution of such power is an obvious inconsistency, understandably challenged by those not in power. It is not my intention to describe and analyse all the major and minor shortcomings of our affluent society, nor to indicate how to remedy these. It will not even be possible to link up all the problems of consumption today with recent developments in the economic theory of consumer behaviour.

For me it is an open question whether it is the explicit duty of scientific activity to improve the human condition or that it is in itself, as such, of value like a piece of art. Still, if, because of our understanding of what is going on, we can suggest improvements, this is all the better. Furthermore, action is sometimes, correctly or incorrectly, justified by an appeal to theoretical conclusions. Let us, therefore, turn now to the theory of consumer demand. Two warnings are in order for the benefit of those that hope for ready-made solutions of actual problems. First: development of pure theory is usually autonomous, only sometimes in response to the possibilities of application and rarely in response to the needs of application. Second: in scientific activity abstraction is a virtue. It is not so much that one abstracts from the complications of reality that matters but more the extent to which the abstraction from certain complications affects the empirical validity of the conclusions. Recent developments display jointly a tendency towards more abstraction and more realism. What Schumpeter said when commenting on the economic profession after 1870 is even more true today: "... economists became more specialized and less accessible to the reading public and because of this economists earned plenty of – entirely unreasonable – reproach not only from spokesman of this public but also from the less technique-minded in their own midst."

2. The Paradigm of Consumption Theory

To see recent developments in their proper perspective it is necessary to go a century back into the past, to what is properly named the "revolution" in economic theory. Around the 1870's emerged what one would nowadays call a *paradigm,* a coherent set of assumptions, accepted by the majority of the profession. A central rôle was attributed to the consumer. By choosing the best among the available alternatives the consumer directs production. He is the sovereign of the economic process. One might qualify this in the sense that he seems to be more a constitutional monarch, with rather limited freedom of action and only a rôle to play in an act written and directed by others. Anyway, however his preferences are formed, the almost tautological principle that the consumer does what he prefers within the limits of his possibilities has turned out to be extremely rich in its implications and as of today its possibilities have not yet been explored to the full. In essence, it is a simple formal optimization model. It has the advantage that apart from its rôle as a descriptive device its methodology can be immediately used for more normative problems.

Technically speaking, our consumer was equipped with a utility function, which he maximized subject to a budget constraint. Since "utility" is a somewhat mysterious concept, later developments took away his utility function and replaced it with an indifference map. For the benefit of the older generation an integrability condition was added so that one could go back from an indifference map to a utility function. Indifference maps or rather indifference curves are convenient expository tools to illustrate the consumer choice problem and although their properties are difficult to interpret, the textbook type of economics is still using them. More recent developments take their starting point in a set of axioms about the preferences. As a first axiom the consumer is supposed to *compare* two alternatives and to state whether he prefers one above the other or not. A second axiom, that of *transitivity,* ensures consistency of choice. These two axioms make it possible to order all possible alternatives according to their ranking in preference.

To go beyond trivial conclusions the preference ordering is assigned a number of properties. First of all the meaning of an ordering of alternatives is narrowed down to an ordering of alternative sets of quantities of goods and services. Furthermore, not all goods and services are relevant for the purpose of formalizing choice behaviour. Goods or

services which the consumer can acquire or consume whatever he wants
without sacrificing any alternative, the well-known free goods, are
dropped from the analysis. For the remaining goods and services it is
assumed that for at least one he can never reach saturation. This is the
property of *desirability*. Another property is that of *convexity* of
preferences. This property means that a convex combination of two
bundles of goods and services, between which the consumer is
indifferent, is preferred to the original bundles. This property becomes
more meaningful in combination with the usually made assumption of
complete *divisibility* of all commodities or services. This divisibility is
not necessarily physical divisibility (think of shared ownership, more or
less used durables and so on). It is less a property of the preferences than
of the alternatives. Another property is that of *substitutability* or
continuity of preferences. This property implies that one can always
compensate a reduction in the quantity of one item in a bundle by an
increase in the quantity of another to obtain an equally desirable bundle.
This property excludes lexicographic preferences, which is less
restrictive than it seems. The two properties last mentioned together
with that of desirability imply that for no scarce good or service
saturation is reached.

If the prices of the scarce goods are given and also the total available
means are given, the bundles that can be acquired by the consumer can
be ranked according to his preferences. The axioms and properties just
given imply that among this set of bundles one and only one is preferred
and will be "demanded." With each income and price situation
corresponds exactly one bundle demanded. The relation between the
quantity of a commodity or service on the one hand and available means
and all prices on the other is called a demand function. These demand
functions are homogeneous of degree zero in all prices and the available
means. Another property of these functions is that the bundle demanded
uses up the complete budget. This means that if the budget is reduced
while the prices remain the same the quantity demanded of at least one
commodity has to be reduced. For some purposes, like certain
propositions of general equilibrium theory these results for the demand
functions are enough. For more specialized demand theory one needs
more.

Another implication of the set of assumptions about the preference
ordering is the possibility to represent it by a mapping to the real line.
This mapping results in a real-valued continuous, monotone increasing

and strictly quasi-concave function in the quantities of the goods and services. It is nothing else than the well-known *utility function*, where "utility" now is simply a name, without any hedonistic connotation. It simply assigns to each bundle a real number such that two equally preferred bundles get the same number and a bundle that is preferred to another bundle is represented by a higher number. As long as this ordering is preserved any method of indexation may be used. Maximizing this utility function subject to the budget results in the same set of demand functions mentioned earlier. The utility function is simply an intermediate step. From such a utility function indifference maps can be derived. The familiar concepts have been more rigorously derived and defined.

In the classical theory utility functions have usually been assumed to be differentiable. *Differentiability of the utility function* is a necessary condition for the differentiability of the demand functions. For many purposes it is attractive to have differentiable demand functions. It is as yet not quite clear what conditions have to be satisfied by the preference ordering to obtain differentiable utility functions, but the assumption of differentiability of the utility function seems not to be overly restrictive, apart from certain corner situations. Differentiability is not enough to arrive at differentiable demand functions. A certain additional smoothness condition has to be added to avoid singularity points.

Although the utility function is only an intermediate step it is still a very convenient tool. Assuming its differentiability one can derive further properties of the demand functions like the decomposition of the effect of small price changes into an *income effect*, i.e. an effect that can be neutralized by an appropriate change in total expenditure, and into a *substitution effect*. Furthermore, the own substitution effect has to be negative. The well-known downward sloping demand curve of the elementary textbooks cannot be derived on the basis of this theory as a universal law. Only if an increase in price is associated with a neutralization of its income effect, i.e. an appropriate increase in total expenditures, will demand for the commodity in question decrease. Recently, interesting results have been reached by a further decomposition of the substitution effect into a *general* one and a *specific* one. The latter is closely related to interactions between goods and services in the preference ordering.

This brief sketch of the basis elements of current demand theory may suffice to set the stage for a discussion of other and further developments. Some of these fit nicely into the existing framework, others show its limitations.

3. Some Related Methodological Issues

The theory as summarized above starts off from preferences, *latent preferences*. Since before the second world war we have an alternative approach commencing with assumptions about demand functions and *revealed preferences*. This approach has been heralded as a "behaviouristic" or "econometric" approach. Instead of making assumptions about potential alternatives, it formulates assumptions about actual, in principle *directly* observable, behaviour. At least in principle, its assumptions could be *directly* verified or, more appropriately speaking, rejected. Curiously enough, this approach has in fact not produced another theory. On the contrary, most of the theoretical research has been directed towards establishing its equivalence with the latent preference approach: the assumptions of the one approach are the conclusions of the other. The two approaches corroborate each other, although the *latent* preference approach is slightly more general because a number of its implications can reveal themselves in situations where there is no market. The revealed preference approach has as yet not been very fruitful for empirical research, contrary to what one had expected when it was first formulated.

The famous *ordinality-cardinality* controversy has occupied generations of economists until this day. The early marginalists were cardinalists. They saw in utility something real, measurable like temperature. Among later generations there were economists that rejected this idea and, consequently, all concepts that were not invariant under order-preserving transformations of the utility function. As the consequence of this an appealing concept like marginal utility was replaced by the rather complicated concept of marginal rate of substitution. Nowadays, the controversy has lost its meaning. All properties of the demand functions are invariant under (differentiable) order-preserving transformations of the utility functions. Restrictions on the demand functions can be based on a certain functionally specified utility function, like the Gossen function, the Bergson function, the Stone-Geary function and so on. These functions lose their simple properties when exposed to non-linear monotone increasing transformations, but the restrictions on the demand functions remain valid. The choice of a certain specification of the utility function implies a number of restrictions on the preference ordering and hence on the demand functions. These are not changed if one starts off from another utility function that represents the same restricted, preference ordering. Cardinality is both unnecessary and harmless. One only has to be careful in the interpretation of certain intermediate results if one uses a cardinal approach.

Two concepts are related to the utility function. The first one is the *indirect utility function*. If one replaces the quantities of goods and services in the utility functions by the demand functions one obtains an expression in all prices and total expenditure. This expression is named the indirect utility function. It assigns to a set of prices and total expenditure the maximum utility to be reached given the budget constraint. The concept is of interest for two reasons. One is that from a given indirect utility function one can by the use of Roy's rule immediately derive proper demand functions. The other is that one can easily derive constant utility price indexes from a given indirect utility function. This price index is a simple ratio. In the denominator one has total expenditure in the reference situation. The numerator is the expenditure needed to obtain the same (maximum) utility level as in the reference situation when the set of price has changed. This amount results from a solution of the indirect utility function with respect to expenditure for the new set of prices and the old utility level. In fact this solution can be expressed as the *expenditure function*, which assigns to a given set of prices and a level of utility associated with a given bundle the minimum expenditure to reach the same level of utility by the bundle demanded. Constant utility price indexes have to be treated with care when applied, as they are usually done, to intertemporal comparisons. One seems to compare an actual bundle in the past with a potential bundle now or vice versa. These bundles relate to two different moments in time and are not alternatives. The correct interpretation is the following: If the prices and expenditure of the past would prevail today, one will demand bundle A today. The constant utility price index then gives the expenditure needed such that for today's prices a bundle B is demanded that is equally desirable as bundle A. The problem is analogous to the one of interpersonal utility comparisons which within the received theory are possible when one resorts to the question: if I am in his conditions would I be better or worse off than I am in my own conditions.

The expenditure function has an interesting methodological aspect. It is the objective function of the dual of the utility maximization problem. There is an obvious *symmetry between demand theory and production theory*. The exact nature of the symmetry is not always well-understood. The ingredients of production theory consist of a production function and a profit function or cost function. Assume that prices are not affected by the producer's behaviour. The primal problem of the producer can be formulated as minimizing costs given a certain level of production. The dual is then to maximize output given total costs. Both approaches lead to the same amounts of inputs, and consequently to the same input demand functions of which there are two equivalent sets. One expresses input demand as a function of input prices and output (the primal set). The second expresses input demand as a function of input prices and total costs (the dual set). The rôles of primal and dual are reversed in consumer demand. The primal problem of the consumer is to maximize utility given total expenditure. The dual problem is to minimize expenditure given a certain level of utility. The set of primal demand functions of the consumer is formally equivalent with the set of dual demand functions of the producer. Unfortunately for the use of this symmetry, in both cases the dual problems are somewhat artificial and therefore less appealing to intuition.

The comparison with production theory leads us naturally to an extension of consumer theory. In the usual production model the producer is assumed to operate both on output and input, on supply and on demand. The usual consumption model concentrates on demand only. This limitation can be easily removed. One simply has to include *time*, one's own time, among the arguments of the utility function. The "price" of this time is what one would receive on the labour market for a unit of time. Total available time is divided between one's own time and market time. Total expenditure is replaced by total time multiplied by the price of time. Otherwise the formal structure is left unchanged. Among the demand functions one has now one that relates one's own time to the prices of all goods and services, including the price of time, and to full-time pay. It is a simple matter to transform this function into a supply of labour function by taking the difference between total time and one's own time. There is a complicating feature in this extension. The price of time is not independent of the amount offered, for example overtime pay is usually higher than normal time pay. Still, the basic ideas can be applied to analyse demand for, say, longer vacations or early retirement.

The approach just mentioned has been further refined by the American *human capital* school. Non-market time can be distinguished into leisure time and household production time. The household production time is used to transform market goods into what one consumes directly. The utility function is then expressed in directly consumable goods and services like a cup of hot tea, watching TV or *dolce far niente*. The transformation functions of market goods and household production time can be substituted for the directly consumable goods and services. One is back to the more classical approach except that one has household production time among the arguments. The interesting aspect of this extension is that one establishes a formal link between household technology and supply of labour on the market. This can be used to explain rising female participation rates and demand for restaurant meals or ready-to-eat food, teabags and so on. This approach comes close to a formalization of the "time is money" slogan. Less down to earth one may say that this approach does more explicitly justice to the fact that time is scarce for mortal beings. This approach has many possibilities. For instance, it can be used to describe the transition of a autarchic household economy to a market economy both in economic history as in development economics. It can also be used to analyse the appearance within a market economy of do-it-yourself activities, which can be explained in part by the difference between gross wages and net wages due to taxation and social security charges. These possibilities have as yet hardly been exploited.

Related to this issue is the controversy between *satisficing* and *maximizing* as far as the consumer is involved. The satisficing hypothesis states that the decision maker will not exert himself in finding out the best solution, but will be content with one which he feels is close enough to the best. Intuitively, he assumes that the difference is not worth his time and other costs of information gathering. The approaches can be reconciled and the controversy can be resolved by explicitly introducing the costs of decision making itself which is usually ignored. In this way one can formulate a simple answer to the question why the average man knows what he wants when he enters a shop and the average woman does not. It is not that the average man is more purposeful than the average woman. It can be simply explained by the fact that in our societies time is still higher priced for the average man than for the average woman. The same answer can be given to the question why women are more price sensitive than men, and why retired people are more price sensitive than people in the active ages.

We will conclude this more or less arbitrary selection of methodological issues related to and within the paradigm of consumer demand by noting that nowhere use is made of the concept of *value*. This contrasts with the past, when micro-economics was called the theory of value, price and income. One obviously does not need a concept like value in economics. In this sense economics has become value-free. At the same time it frees this concept from an economic connotation and clears the way for a proper evaluation of the importance of economics.

4. The Structure and Formation of Preferences

In the view of some, preferences are a datum for economic theory and consequently need not to be further analysed by economists. Intuitively it is clear that preferences are changed by economic variables, and that some knowledge about the structure of preferences can be used to formulate constraints on demand and, the other way around, observations on demand behaviour can lead to some insight into the structure of preferences. It is also not true that economists have not occupied themselves with formulating hypotheses about preferences. It suffices to refer to the hypothesis of decreasing time preference.

In recent years this analysis of preferences has made considerable progress. We will first discuss here the implications of *separability of the preference ordering*. There is an intuitive notion that some goods are more related to each other than to other goods. One can form groups of goods and services that have such strong interrelations. For example, for a number of purposes it seems not unreasonable to treat the 200 or so different varieties of cheese as one single group: cheese. Grouping can be done on the basis of physical or psychological similarity. The set of all possible goods and services is correspondingly decomposed into subsets. Given the quantities of all goods and services outside a certain subset one can order the combinations of the quantities within the subset according to one's preferences. If this order is not changed when the rest of the bundle changes one speaks of separable preferences. Its implications are easy to establish. Given the prices of the items of such a subset and what to spend on them one can immediately determine the quantities demanded of this subset. One has demand functions in terms of only the prices of this subset and the outlay on this subset. These demand functions display the same properties as the ones for the complete set. What will be spent on this subset is a function of total available means and the set of price indexes for the groups. Individual prices enter the picture here only indirectly by means of their impact on the price index of the group. In the case of *strongly* separable preferences one does not even need the price indexes for the other groups to explain expenditure on a certain group, but only a general price index for all items outside this group.

The implications of separability are very attractive. To study, say, the demand for margarine and butter, one has not to worry about the prices of shoelaces or toothpaste. Furthermore, one can distinguish whole hierarchies of groups. In this connection one speaks of *utility trees:* the complete set is the trunk, major subsets are the branches, and so on until one has come to the items, the leaves. The separability hypothesis is very fruitful for theoretical as well as empirical research.

An important application of this hypothesis is the following. Let the goods and services be distinguished according to the period of consumption: a loaf of bread today is essentially different from a loaf of bread tomorrow. Assume that it is reasonable to group consumption items according to the periods distinguished such that the preference ordering is separable in these groups. There are two levels of decision-making. The first level consists in determining how total means are to be allocated over the various periods. Given this allocation one determines how the means for each period will be allocated over the items per period. The first level of decision-making is the subject of the *theory of the consumption function,* where all kinds of intertemporal elements enter the analysis, like interest rates, price and income expectations, life expectancy, future needs and so on. The second level of decision-making is studied in *the theory of the demand functions,* where one only needs to know total expenditure for a certain period and the prices for that period. The separability hypothesis justifies to make abstraction of the actual pattern of consumption if one studies the relation between income and spending, and to abstract from all kinds of intertemporal relationships if one is studying the actual pattern of consumption today. It is not my intention to give an account of developments in the field of the theory of the consumption function. I only mention that efforts have been made to integrate the permanent income hypothesis with the life-cycle hypothesis. Furthermore, the impact of structured uncertainty on the consumption-savings decision has been studied. What is as yet lacking is a more fundamental treatment of declining time preference, which is no doubt related with uncertainty and attitudes towards risk.

A further aspect of contemporaneous separability is a simple structure of the cross substitution effects of price changes for items belonging to different groups. In this connection it is useful to return for a moment to the distinction of the substitution effect into a specific and a general one. In the case that the preference ordering is strongly separable in the commodities, obviously a limiting case, the specific cross substitution effect vanishes, while the specific own substitution effect is proportional to the effect of a change in income. The general substitution effect reflects an intertemporal allocation effect and the distinction between specific and general substitution effects remains valid even if there is no contemporaneous separability, although it loses its importance for empirical work.

It may be doubted that it is possible to come to a distinction of all possible goods and services into non-overlapping groups. Still, it is desirable to structure the preferences in one way or another. On the basis of empirical studies one may construct possibly overlapping groups that behave as if they were strongly separable. These groups should correspond with basic needs, which are more or less independent of each other. This approach logically requires that there are as many basic needs as there are elementary goods and services. Related to this approach but independently developed, is the idea that preferences are generated because of the existence of some basic needs, like hunger, thirst, prestige or love. The satisfaction of these needs can be produced by a function of quantities of a particular subset of goods and services. The ordering of the preferences among goods and services results then from the combination of the ordering of the basic needs and these production functions. It is clear that there is some formal relation with the approach of the human capital school and its household production functions. As yet it is not quite clear what the fundamental needs are. To be fundamental they should be in some sense independent. This approach offers an attractive opportunity of joint research by psychologists and economists. As far as I know, such a joint effort has not been undertaken. Although purchasing behaviour has on more incidental basis been analysed by psychologists, there is as yet no complete theory of demand based on a set of hypotheses about fundamental motivations.

The approach just mentioned has the advantage that by leaving the ordering of needs unchanged new goods and services can be introduced, i.e. the production functions can be changed, resulting in a change in the ordering of preferences among goods and services. I should add that as yet no systematic effort has been made to analyse the changing preference ordering from this point of view. Actually, certain types of changes in the preference ordering don't constitute a particular problem for the theory of demand outlined above. The preference ordering can be made conditional on the values of variables other than the composition of the bundles. An obvious example is the weather, or one's physical condition. As these variables change, so will the preference ordering and, as a consequence, demand. It can be shown that the impact of these changes is related to the substitution effect of prices. A successful campaign to promote the drinking of milk has an effect proportional to the substitution effect of a decrease in the price of milk. It will increase the consumption of milk and decrease demand for at least some other items. In the same way one can analyse the effects of more information, which could either work positively or negatively on demand for certain goods and services.

In general one can distinguish three types of causes of changes of preferences, which fit in this framework. One group is made up out of all causes outside human control. The second one finds its origin in the behaviour of others, like one's neighbours, advertising firms, one's own and other national states. The third type reflects one's own behaviour. If one is not interested in the identification of these causes one may treat their effects on the preference ordering as a random variable. One can also concentrate on one or more of these causes.

It is perhaps useful to discuss somewhat more in detail certain of these causes. The effect of weather conditions on demand for beer is well-known. Not so well-known is what goods or services are less in demand to pay for the extra beer during a heat wave. "Keeping-up with the Jones" makes the preference ordering dependent on the behaviour by the Jones. This social cause of change in preferences is no doubt one of the most effective. Still, apart from such exceptions like the relative income hypothesis, it has as yet not been integrated in the theory of demand functions. In fact, entirely different models, diffusion models, have been used to explain demand for appliances, where the social component seems to be dominant. One should distinguish between a mere sociological aspect and the information aspect. Seeing neighbour Jones at work with his new appliance is one of the easiest ways to find out how desirable it could be for your own use. Wanting to have something because Jones has it, is an entirely different matter.

Recently, attention has been given to the impact of one's own behaviour in the past on one's preferences now. It provides one way to obtain a dynamic version of demand behaviour. Past purchasing behaviour can result in stocks. These stocks are not necessarily physical. In fact, they are psychological stocks and can be positive or negative. Positive stocks of a good reduce its desirability, negative stocks increase its desirability. A hangover is an example of a positive stock. Negative stocks are related to items to which one gets addicted like cigarettes, books, drugs. Part of this can be attributed to an effect of "learning by doing", part of this is a purely physiological effect, while there is also a simple physical aspect to this matter. Theoretically, one can handle the effect of past demand by including it among the explanatory variables in the demand functions. On a practical level this has to be structured in a relatively restricted way to be able to do any measurement at all. Under such restrictions interesting results have been obtained.

To conclude this, too brief, sketch of what is going on in the analysis of the structure and formation of preferences, I would like to state explicitly what is already implied in the foregoing: the analysis of preferences is an important and vital aspect of demand theory. Preferences are changed not only by factors outside the economic process, but by the nature of the economic process itself. Recent work shows that economists are realizing this more and more.

5. Some Other Issues

It would be unreasonable to expect that the paradigm of demand theory can cope equally well with all possible issues that turn up in the analysis of consumer demand. A discussion of some topics for which as yet the paradigm does not seem to be too fruitful in the sense of producing elegant and useful results might show some of its limitations.

As mentioned earlier, the axiom of substitutability or continuity of preferences excludes lexicographic orderings. A lexicographic ordering is a hierarchical concept. The goods and services are divided into subsets. These subsets are ordered in the sense that more of the first subset is always preferred to some of the first subset and some of the second one and so on. Under normal conditions a consumer will never go outside the first subset and within a static framework one can adequately limit the validity of the theory to this first subset only. This means, however, that the preference ordering is defined on different subsets for different individuals. Some people will never consume alcoholics or Brussels sprouts, but others do. For the non-consumers these goods have no desirability at all. Otherwise said, for each consumer there are goods and services of which he does not perceive their desirability. He might know of the existence of these goods or not. They may be even goods that as yet do not exist. However, for one reason or the other the consumer's perception of their desirability might change. This means that the subset of goods and services on which the preference ordering is defined changes. This causes a serious discontinuity raising a number of methodological problems, that are not easily remedied. For practical purposes these problems are especially relevant when new goods and services are introduced. One way out of these problems is to let the preference ordering pertain to all goods and services, including not yet existing ones and to assign to the goods and services outside the first subset an arbitrarily small desirability, implying an arbitrarily small demand for them. However, this is not a very elegant way to deal with, say, the emergence of new goods. Preferences with respects to those new goods tend to change very fast and one has to acknowledge that other models, like diffusion models, are more flexible tools to describe the development of demand for new goods than the more classical demand functions.

Another set of problems is caused by the assumption of complete divisibility. Many durables are characterized by a certain degree of lumpiness. To consider the services they render as the final commodity does ignore the desirability of the convenience and social prestige derived from pure ownership. For the purposes of empirical research one tends to develop ownership models rather than the more traditional demand functions to explain purchasing of durables. However, it can be shown that for aggregate demand over a number of individuals the complications of the indivisible nature of durables are reduced and tend to vanish.

This leads us to the problems of aggregation over individuals. As Hicks puts it somewhat too strongly the behaviour of an actual individual person "does not deserve a moment's consideration" of the economist. Economists are mostly concerned with aggregate or average behaviour. The paradigm is, however, completely about an individual. In one sense this is not a grave problem. One simply adds up individual demand to aggregate demand. In another sense this is not very satisfactory. The individual demand functions display a number of attractive properties. Can these properties be imposed on aggregate demand relations? There seems not too much of a problem for the homogeneity, symmetry and negativity conditions, but there are serious problems for the effect of income changes and the income effect of price changes. These can be overcome by postulating certain restrictive conditions on the distribution of real income. Then one has "nice" aggregate demand functions. Under these conditions one can even postulate the existence of an aggregate utility function, which, of course, is not a representation of a collective preference ordering, which is a meaningless concept, but more a convenient methodological device. One is back to the "representative consumer". This device has, moreover, the advantage that there is no need to distinguish between socially generated changes in preferences and changes in preferences resulting from the individual consumer's own behaviour. Still, it is only valid under rather restrictive conditions about which not much empirical evidence is available.

Another series of problems is related to the rôle of the well-being of others in one's preference ordering. There is as yet not a well-developed theory of the economics of philanthropy or social responsability. On an abstract level one can solve this problem by considering expected actual demand bundles of others as parameters of the preference ordering of the individual and hence as parameters of the utility function. Solidarity corresponds with a positive interaction. If the means are shared one has the ingredients necessary to analyse the economics of a consumers' commune. Under what conditions is equilibrium and harmony possible? This question has as yet not been given much attention. Another aspect of this approach is that in view of the possibility to change the preference ordering preferences can be influenced towards more or less solidarity. How to achieve this is more a matter for the specialists in the field of education and mass media than for the economists. The rôle of the economist would be to study the economic consequences of such changes.

As a last example of types of problems that are not explained well by the use of the paradigm or have received no systematic attention, I would like to mention the following. If preferences can be changed they can also be changed by conscious, intentional actions of the consumer himself, but what would motivate such an action is not clear. It is puzzling to be able to analyse, at least in principle, the motivations for unintentional actions that change the preference ordering, while not to have even the beginning of an answer for the motivations of their intentional counterparts.

6. Empirical Studies

A description of trends in demand analysis cannot leave out developments in empirical demand studies. Empirical studies of demand behaviour have a long tradition. For a long time these studies have been almost completely unrelated with theory. They were also very much *ad hoc,* trying to describe demand for one particular item. It is not my intention to describe all possible ways to conduct empirical demand studies. I will concentrate on those studies that are more closely related to the theory. Furthermore, I will only briefly mention studies based on cross-sectional information. Although cross-sections of household budgets are a goldmine for the researcher, the possibility to study the effect of price changes is hampered by the almost non-existent price variation in the period for which the data are gathered. Hence they are less attractive for the purpose of studying demand behaviour. On the other hand, in budget analysis it is relatively easy to take into account the effects of social class, physical environment, family size and the like. It is then implicitly assumed that households in the same conditions have the same preferences apart from a random component. However, empirical evidence shows that very frequently certain households don't buy certain items at all, which might reflect that preferences are more essentially different. Methods have been developed to estimate Engel curves, *i.e.* the relations between expenditure on an item and total income, taking into account such essential differences but only up to a certain degree.

   Here, I will describe in more detail empirical analysis of demand functions, as relations between the quantity demanded on the one hand and total means and all prices on the other. The data are usually of an aggregate nature referring to demand and prices for a country during an annual period. Only aggregate behaviour can therefore be studied. This study can be done for two purposes. One is to check on the results of the theory. The other is to arrive at a complete description of demand for all items or groups of items. Both types of studies face a number of problems in common of which I will now mention some.

First, one has to be convinced that aggregate demand functions are valid descriptions of aggregate demand behaviour. There are here some *problems of aggregation* already mentioned. Secondly, the old *identification* question has to be answered in a positive sense to avoid a distortion due to supply behaviour. Next one has to choose a *functional form* that is realistic, manageable and consistent with theory. The well-known specification with constant income and price elasticities is realistic, but not consistent with theory. Then, one has to solve the problem of *dimensionality*. Assume that one has only 100 goods and services. The quantities demanded have each to be related to 100 prices plus total means. Without making use of theoretical constraints and assumptions about the "collective" utility function one needs at least 100 observations for each variable to estimate the simplest function. These are rarely available and even if they are estimation will require the inversion of a matrix of 101 x 101, which is even for a modern fast computer still a considerable task. To reduce the dimensionality problem one usually constructs a limited number of groups of goods and services. In most of the empirical studies from 4 to 16 groups have been used. This procedure is legitimate if the utility function is indeed weakly separable in these groups. Anyway such grouping is required to overcome the problem of limited availability of data. There will be still a serious *degree of freedom* problem. To deal with this, the theoretical constraints like the homogeneity condition and the symmetry condition are helpful. There is still a *computational difficulty.* In one of my experiments with a system of sixteen demand functions matrices of 105 x 105 had to be inverted. Nowadays a fast computer with a large core memory can handle this adequately, but until a few years ago it was a far from trivial problem. A further reduction in the dimensionality can be obtained by assuming strong separability among the groups.

Most of the empirical demand systems covering more than a few groups make indeed use of this *strong separability* or additivity assumption. Some use instead the assumption of additivity of the indirect utility function. A popular system is the Linear Expenditure System, which explains expenditure on groups as a linear function of total expenditure and prices, but which is non-linear in the coefficients. The system implies strong separability. There are many other systems. Comparative studies of empirical performance of these systems are rather inconclusive in the sense that no system clearly dominates the other under equally strong assumptions about the nature of the interactions between the goods and services. A problem with the additivity assumption is that it seems plausible if one works with a small number of major groups, where one does not really need it, and that it seems implausible if one has a system for a large number of groups, where one needs it.

The disadvantage of the incorporation of constraints in the estimation procedure is that one cannot test their empirical validity. In general, not too much attention has been paid to the empirical validity of the implications of the theory. Only recently, less than 10 years ago, tests of the theoretical propositions have begun. An excuse of this tardiness is no doubt the lack of adequate computer equipment until a few years ago. Furthermore, the number of rather tentative assumptions one has to make to test, say, the homogeneity and symmetry conditions is considerable and could, if incorrect, invalidate the test. From the tests performed it appears that the relatively weak and almost natural homogeneity condition has to be rejected. The symmetry condition, which is much stronger and actually only based on the assumption of differentiability of the utility function, appears to be less objectionable, but has usually still to be rejected. Strong separability turns out to be too strong, as expected. These are rather negative conclusions, but one should heed the *caveat* made before. Much might depend on the other untested assumptions. The introduction of dynamic elements in such systems, which is a current research topic, might change the picture.

The interesting aspect of the empirical analysis of demand systems is its close tie with the theory of consumer demand. In this respect this branch of applied econometrics is ahead of others where the specifications are more based on rules of thumb than on an explicitly formulated optimization theory. Also in applied econometrics the demonstration effect is at work and in production analysis systems of demand for production factors are now being estimated and tested.

7. Evaluation

From this brief and unavoidably superficial survey it is clear that demand analysis is far from being a closed chapter. The structure to be built on the foundations laid a century ago is not finished at all. Although certain issues of importance cannot be handled elegantly by the basic model it is so flexible that it can be used for still a long time ahead. There are no symptoms to detect the emergence of a new paradigm, or basic model. If demand analysis is not able to produce the answers to a number of questions related to the quality of life today, this is not so much a shortcoming of the basic structure of the theory, but primarily due to a lack of exploiting all its possibilities.

Remarks on the three macro-economics

J. Pen

•

Today I am lecturing on one of my most favourite subjects: the distinction between classical, monetary and Keynesian macro-economics. This distinction is reflected in the history of the Economics Department at the University of Groningen. When the department was founded, and this was as late as the fifties, monetary theory was still the dominant mode of thought; this is true for the Netherlands in general, where the influence of Holtrop and Koopmans was strong, but in particular for Groningen. Monetary equilibrium, the neutrality of money, whether the two are identical (they are not), these were the topics of the day. Keynes came later, at a time when the classical revival was on its way, and when he did so he came in monetary disguise. He looked like Robertson. This method of presenting Keynesian theory in terms of Robertsonian period analysis or even in a terminology à la Koopmans is formally correct, but misses the point that the monetary school, including Robertson, was out to show that the Keynesian revolution either did not exist or was about minor, if not futile, issues. It is true that models can be constructed that absorb both Keynesian and monetary thinking and that even the classical point of view can be incorporated but we should not overlook the ideological implications of the various schools. We can be too tolerant and non-directive in our models and for that reason I wish to stress some of the *differences* between the schools this morning.

The formal differences between monetary and Keynesian theory are as follows. Monetary theory is fond of multiplication – a stock, or an addition to a stock, is multiplied by a velocity. It is of minor importance whether this velocity is seen as a constant, or as a variable to be determined by other variables: price expectations, the rate of interest, methods of payment, degree of "differentiation" within the "business column". The flow of money, or the income stream, or total spending, is seen as a product. Keynesian theory runs primarily in terms of addition or subtraction of income and spending components. Here products and quotients, especially the latter, are used as constants or semi-constants. These quotients (multipliers) are found by comparing flows, but every Keynesian model starts with national income seen as a *sum*. The debate about the relative constancy of velocity versus multipliers looks like an empirical matter, but it follows from the deeper proclivities of the adherents of the two schools: the monetarists see money as a driving force, the Keynesians as a soft quantity that accomodates itself to the needs of firms and households. Therefore, Keynesians are not at all convinced by any empirical "proof" of the constancy of the velocity of circulation; they interpret this type of constancy by assuming that banks do their business in such a way that liquidity preferences are accommodated to the needs of $C + I + G$.

A second, and more important difference between monetary and Keynesian theory is that the Keynesian approach is fascinated by the way in which spending creates income and income creates spending. Equilibrium is reached when the national income generates a sum of expenditure that equals the income; this is Keynesian theory summed up in sixteen words. This basic idea has remained with us, but it has been supplemented by all kinds of other neo-Keynesian relationships. For instance, income distribution may enter the consumption function; indeed, separate consumption functions may be written down for workers and for "capitalists". Exports depend on the wage level, and therefore the wage level may influence employment (which was originally an anti-Keynesian idea), government expenditure may be influenced by tax revenue or by the budget deficit. Investment may be influenced by anything; by superliquidity, even by relative prices of the factors of production, a typical classical notion. Also the production function may be introduced into a Keynesian model and when such a function is introduced its derivatives are not far away. Indeed, the Keynesian approach has become so elastic that it has swallowed both classical and monetary theory. If we compare this broadmindedness with the narrow set-up of the monetary equations, most monetary models look very meagre indeed.

The various models stimulate their own type of quantitative research. Classical theory has a long econometric standing: the work of Cobb and Douglas, and an enormous amount of energy is still devoted to the search for the parameters of the production function, the elasticities of substitution between labour and capital and between types of labour.

Empirical work in monetary theory also produced remarkable results (in particular the work of Friedman and Schwartz). Yet, in my opinion the Keynesian school has been the most fruitful of the three. It started with small models, which concentrate the mind upon a few strategic "propensities" but it ended with the big econometric systems, which spread our attention in a non-directive way. This type of research produces results in various fields: consumption behaviour, investment behaviour, the balance of payments. However, this tolerance has its price. The tiny models of the monetary school imply a theory in the sense of Popper; the Keynesian approach is just an approach, not a welldefined theory. Among modern neo-Keynesians of the broad-minded type (this description does not include Mr. Kaldor and his Cambridge partizans) almost anything is possible. Quantitative research may degenerate into the garbage-in − garbage-out type. And there is the danger of overdeterminateness. In the case of income distribution this point becomes particularly topical; one cannot assert that in a dynamic sense marginal productivity, at a given level of employment, determines the wage rate, and at the same time that marginal productivity determines, at a given wage rate, employment. Static equilibrium systems conceal our view on what is relevant in society. And one cannot of course assert that in a Keynesian system investment always fills the gap between productive capacity on the one hand and consumption and government expenditure on the other hand. That would be a return to narrow-minded classical theory. But this is not the real danger, because we all know that investment does not behave in that way. The real danger is that these tolerant neo-Keynesian models may mask the fact that we have no specific theory of investment at all − a crucial hole in our macro-economics, so that we are left with the agnostic impression that investments are determined by an unknown quantity called Animal Spirits. Finally the trouble with big models is that they are ravenously hungry for parameters. But all the same, my preference is obviously on the side of Keynesian thinking.

I have no sympathy for the neo-Keynesians of the Cambridge School. I reject their criticism of capital theory, in particular their circularity argument, put forward by Mrs. Robinson; there is no reason why not to measure the amount of capital by its (corrected) historical cost. On the other hand, classical theory may be criticized for not having a decent theory of profits. The most penetrating theory of income distribution is the neo-classical, but there is a definite gap in it. We do not understand what exactly determines the level of normal and abnormal profits. This is one of the failures of modern macro-economics; in this sense the theory of distribution is a leaky bucket, though that is better than no bucket at all. It is also true that we do not understand the exact influence of profits, among the other possible determinants, on investment. So it is understandable that economists in Cambridge and elsewhere have been looking for a theory that brings profits, wages and investment together in a small determinate model. But unfortunately the specific Cambridge theory itself with its Widow's Cruse and its two different rates of saving is a useful example of economic nonsense, useful in the sense that it can be used in teaching students what may happen if we rely on identities and confuse them with significant assertions about causes and effects. What we need in its place is a theory of the inflationary spiral; how profits behave in this context, and what the spiral does to investment. This is an unsolved and strategic problem in economics. The weak side of Keynesian economics lies at the supply side, but this can be remedied, as recent research in Groningen (Dr. Kuipers) has shown. Supply comes in by way of the production function. Not by selling ourselves to Harrod – Domar equations; they are seductive, but although I must confess that I had once fallen for them, we can only conclude that they lead us astray. The fixed proportions give an exaggerated idea of the instability of the national income. If Harrod – Domar models were realistic the stable development of the last twenty-five years would have been impossible. Moreover, if we believe in fixed proportions our understanding of income distribution as a phenomenon explained by relative scarcity goes down the drain. A cautious belief in the good old classical theory is much more fruitful. In this respect neo-classical growth theory has a lot of merits. Moreover, the riddles of the Abramowitz Residual and the constant capital-output ratio are perfectly and simultaneously solved once we understand the neo-classical position that the increase in labour productivity is determined by technical progress as well as by the change in capital intensity. The funny fact that the rate of savings disappears from this classical formula makes the whole business even more intriguing.

Though I depict myself as a Keynesian who had embraced classical theory, I also see a definite place for monetary thinking. Within the purely national context this place is usually modest; only in pathological situations money becomes a dominant, driving force. But this is different once the international scene is taken into account. Here the practical problems and the theoretical issues loom up very large. Economists should probably devote more time to these international issues; they should not be left to the purely monetary specialists and to those who are acquainted with international high finance. I am glad to refer these problems to Dr. Södersten. But the possibility of a monetary crisis will be with us for the coming years. There are no easy solutions for that.

Finally, a watershed in economic thinking can be observed. The word "watershed" had been brought up by Dr. Simon, when he referred to the history of the University of Groningen. I am referring to the work of Forrester and Meadows. In my opinion the limits to growth will prove to be one of the greatest theoretical issues of the coming years. Selective growth, the choice of sectors in which further growth should be stopped or become negative; possibly zero growth; its influence on employment (positive or negative?); the political and social conditions for selective growth, these are the great challenges to economic thought in the near future. Economic policy should aim at unusual combinations of goals, like full employment, monetary stability and a cleaner world.

The type of research that is in order to understand these problems should be given priority. This is the new awareness in economics; in this sense the work of Meadows and his team constitutes a real watershed in the history of economic thought.

Between the sound and the simple-minded

Some Reflections on the Methodology
of International Trade Theory

B. Södersten

I will not, in this lecture, try to survey the whole area of international economics. Apart from the fact that this would not be possible during the amount of time alotted to me, several excellent surveys have been published in fairly recent years. I will, however, dwell on some important aspects of the development of international economics during the last 25 years. I will also try to evaluate briefly some of the criticisms against economic theory in general and the theory of international economics in particular which scientists working inside the field of economics and even working outside that field have voiced.

At the core of international economics is the pure theory of international trade, a type of theory that is in many ways very typical of economic theory in general. It works at a high level of abstraction. It tries, as it were, to erect a simplified, self-contained body of theory characterized by the feature of general equilibrium; *i.e.* it tries to picture in a simplified form, *all* the variables which are of importance for the problem at hand.

By a happy coincidence the paper containing the proof of one of the important theorems of the pure theory of trade, Paul Samuelson's paper on factor price equalization, was published in the same year as the Faculty of Economics at Groningen was founded. This is a natural starting point for some comments on static trade theory.

The factor price equalization theorem demonstrates that under free trade, disregarding transport costs and other impediments to trade, factor prices will be equalized. It builds on some rather stringent assumptions, the most interesting and important of which are concerned with the production side of the trading economies. It assumes that production functions are homogeneous of degree one, that there is a unique relationship between prices of goods and prices of factors (no factor reversals) and that production functions are the same in all countries; it is assumed, in other words, that knowledge travels freely;

and that all entrepreneurs in the world have access to the same knowledge.

Samuelson's 1948 paper on factor price equalization started a very intense discussion on various theoretical aspects of the basic static trade model, the so-called Heckscher-Ohlin trade model. During the next ten years several hundreds of papers were published in the leading economic journals with several books to follow suit.

The results of these investigations are primarily of an analytical nature. The understanding of comparative advantage in trade and the implications of general equilibrium have been greatly enhanced. These results tend to be of a definite kind, given the very restrictive nature of the assumptions which are at the bottom of this analysis. This holds at least within the confines of the standard two-by-two-by-two trade model; if complications like several countries, several factors of production, intermediate goods *etc.* are added, further explorations should be possible. From an analytical point of view the high tide of interest in these problems characteristic of the 1950's and early 60's has now receded.

The propositions generated by the static trade theory have also been subject to a certain amount of empirical testing. This line of enquiry was started by a pioneering paper by Wassily Leontief published in 1954. Leontief found that United States' export pattern did not follow the proposals of the Heckscher-Ohlin theory. Leontief's findings sparked off an intense debate. Several countries have since had the international structure of their economies investigated.

Static trade theory has been heavily criticized. Joan Robinson claims for instance: "There is no branch of economics in which there is a wider gap between orthodox doctrine and actual problems than in the theory of international trade".[1]

There is ample scope for criticism of trade theory. Much of the criticism which has been levied against trade theory is, however, not well taken. Trade theory is a fast-growing body of theory of quite a diverse nature. Criticism against trade theory often sounds as if the only type of trade theory which existed was the static part of trade theory. Joan Robinson claims for instance: "The analysis conducted in terms of stationary states leaves out development, accumulation and technical change." This is hardly a correct description of modern trade theory. As

---

1. J. Robinson (3, 1973).

I soon will return to, one of the most interesting parts of modern trade theory is the theory of growth and trade.

One important aspect in evaluating the criticism of trade theory has to do with how one views the place of general equilibrium theory in economics.

Trade theory is essentially a branch of general equilibrium analysis. It is firmly embedded in the Walrasian tradition. From there stems the preoccupation with creating a theory that is self-contained, where all variables of importance enter and where all variables are interdependent.

Such a theory will of necessity be of an abstract and simplified nature. It works with a few well-defined variables and relies on simplyfying assumptions, some of which are of a drastic nature. Its strength lies in the fact that it creates a picture of the world which in important ways is complete.

An important line in the criticism of trade theory is really not aimed so much at trade theory *per se* as it is aimed at general equilibrium theory in general. At the heart of general equilibrium theory are the notions of determinateness and completeness: the relations which describe an economy must form a complete whole where all the variables of the system can be determined. The viewpoint that all factors which make up an economy hang together and are dependent on each other has had a very strong place in economic theorizing. It might even be said to have been *the* distinctive feature of economics as a science. It had also had important policy implications as it has forced policy makers to try to view the economy as a whole and not simply try to focus the attention on the effect of a parameter change on one or two obvious variables. At the same time it must be admitted that the concentration on general equilibrium theory has very heavily stressed rigour and formal elegance at the expense of interpretations of theory, of testing of hypotheses and of comparisons of the assertions of theory with reality.

My own personal point of view is somewhat divided but on the whole I would like to argue in favor of general equilibrium theorizing. I think the general equilibrium approach has brought significant results within the field of international economics. Less so, perhaps, in the purely static part of trade theory than in the area of comparative statics, which after all, contains the bulk of trade theory. I will soon try to elaborate and clarify my point of view in these matters.

Before doing so I would, however, like to make an observation on the logic of scientific development.

Much of the work on static trade theory in the 50's and early 60's can, according to my view, be explained in terms of the internal development of the subject. When the Heckscher-Ohlin model began to be studied more seriously, the full structure of the model was hardly discernable, many loose ends were left and several generalizations remained to be done.

Scientific theory does not like vacuum nor does it like dark corners. The logic of scientific development demands that the full implication of a theoretical structure be explored. After a certain amount of time such an undertaking might lead to decreasing returns to scale. This usually does not stop the logical development of a subject from going its way. This holds for economics as well as for other sciences with a well-developed body of theorems.

The role of the notion of general equilibrium in trade theory is debatable. The strongest criticism which can be raised against static trade theory is, however, according to my view, of quite a different nature. It has to do with the role of assumptions in neoclassical economic theory.

In order to make my point clear in this connection I would like to make the distinction between the basic methodology of neoclassical economics and its assumptions. One of the perceptions that has greatly muddled the controversy about the applicability of the neoclassical paradigm to contemporary economic problems has been the confusion of the basic methodology of the paradigm with its assumptions. One is often given the impression that they are joint goods: one must accept either both or neither.

I think this is wrong. It is eminently possible to subscribe to the basically sound methodological apparatus of neoclassical economics without accepting some of its debatable assumptions. The assumption of free competition, to take an example, and its corollary, the disregard of possibilities of collusion, has in many instances had very harmful effects on the realism of the results of theory. It is often quite absurd to believe that a company operating in a development context would fail to take into consideration the effects of its operations on the local power structure and income distribution.

In the same vein it will recognize the importance of the international power structure that is often a prerequisite for its profitable operations and long-run survival. I might here refer to the activities in international politics by firms like ITT, United Fruit and the big oil companies.[2]

2. A description of the political activities of the world's largest corporation, ITT, can be found in the recent book by Anthony Sampson.

The restrictive and simple-minded assumptions which are at the basis of static trade theory, like the factor price equalization theorem, have been harmful in at least three ways. The first has to do with the static approach of the theory. The results of the factor price equalization theorem can hardly be viewed as applicable to any real world situation even in the so-called long run (whatever that means) as it is contradictory to apply a static model to long-run analysis in a changing world. The second assumption which has had harmful effects has to do with the disregard of possibilities of collusion.

It is highly probable that firms will observe that they can collude and thereby increase their power in the market and turn the income distribution in favor of capital and management; this might be especially important in the context of developing countries. This implies that firms are not only maximizing absolute profits but that they also maximize their influence by control of relative shares which affects power relationships. In the same manner there are strong incentives for firms to collude in order to reduce uncertainty. The third has to do with power in an international context. By influencing international politics, for instance by trying to influence and perhaps even bribe politicians both in the home and the guest countries the large international corporations can reduce potential sources of competition and threats to nationalizations *etc.* and thereby steer market forces to its advantage.

Static trade theory, for instance in the form of the factor price equalization theorem, should not, according to my view, primarily be viewed as giving a realistic picture of the world or as being strongly geared to empirical testing. It gives us, however, indispensable tools and insights into the general equilibrium nature of trading economies. I will now go on and deal with some theorems in comparative static trade theory which are of considerable interest both from a theoretical and practical point of view. It would, however, have been difficult to develop these kind of theorems except against the background of static trade theory.

Economic growth has, from a historical point of view, been very rapid in the era since World War II. Growth has also, up to very recent years, been of overriding concern to most governments and politicians. Economics is a science very sensitive to changing fashions. Economists want very much to be useful. They are easily duped and prone to become scientific opportunists. When politicians were high on growth, the theory of economic growth became the highest fashion within economics.

This fashion had important repercussions for the development of international economic theory. A seminal paper by John Hicks published in 1953 was the starting-point for the modern theory of economic growth and international trade. This type of theory treated basically economic growth as an exogeneous factor, though it was careful in distinguishing between various sources of growth, which were of special importance when technical progress was the growth-inducing factor. It then studied the effects of growth on trade.

From a methodological point of view this theory used a comparative-static approach. There is little doubt about that the most interesting results in the pure theory of trade are derived by comparative-static methods. The bulk of the analytical literature also uses such methods.

This part of trade theory again uses a general equilibrium framework. But there is no longer the question of studying only characteristics of a given general equilibrium situation. A change is introduced and the effects of that change on the variables in the model are then studied.

The theory of growth and trade is a very typical example of the development of international economic theory in the 1950's and 60's. Hicks took a very broad view in his paper. He used what was in essence a two country-three sector model and his primary aim was to explain the dollar shortage of Western Europe that existed in the late 40's and early 50's. But he meant that his model also was flexible enough to explain the decline of ancient Rome and the downfall of Venice as a center for Europe's trade with the East in the sixteenth century.

At the core of Hicks' analysis lay productivity changes between export and import lines. Hicks introduced the terms export-biased and import-biased productivity changes. He suggested that the reason for Europe's difficulties was that economic growth in the United States had changed from being export-biased in the 19th century to become import-biased and that this had led to worsening of the terms of trade and deficits in the balance of payments for Europe.

Hicks' analysis was sketchy and incomplete, for instance in its omission of the demand side. Soon, however, a great many papers and, later on, some books followed and the effects of growth on trade became greatly clarified.

The analysis dealt with two main cases: the effects of factor accumulation and the effects of technical progress. The effects of factor accumulation centers around the so-called Rybczynski theorem. This established, by an ingenious use of geometry, that if capital (to take an example) accumulates, the relative price of the capital-intensive product would have to fall and that of the labor-intensive product would have to increase; if commodity prices were to be kept unchanged it implied that production of the good intensive in the non-augmenting factor would have to decline in absolute terms. These results were powerful, they were far from being trivial and then have later on been widely used in various investigations. Further analysis, using full-scale algebraic methods, have proven, however, that they are critically dependent on production functions being homogeneous of degree one.

The effects of technical progress were also analysed. Here Hicks' classifications of innovations into neutral, labor- and capital-saving introduced in the early 1930's were restated and used anew. It turned out that the simplest case, in which the neutral innovation increases the marginal productivity of both factors of production, had clearcut results. In this case technical progress in the export sector would always turn the terms of trade against the innovating country. This implied that the progressing country would always have to export away some of the fruits of its inventions to its trading partners. How large the effects on prices and volumes would be depended then on income and demand elasticities and on substitution possibilities on the supply side. These results were derived using very weak assumptions regarding the production side. It was demonstrated that clear, qualitative results could be reached even with the use of unspecified production functions.[3] The important factors were the change in the production function and the changes in marginal productivities connected with technical progress. As long as both the marginal productivity of labor and capital in the two-factor model increased because of technical progress the terms of trade would deteriorate if the export sector was the innovating sector and improve if the import-competing sector was the innovating one. If however, the marginal productivity of one factor fell in connection with technical progress the upshot for the development of prices and volumes became less determinate and was to hinge on the relative strength of the absolute changes in marginal productivities and the change in the production function itself.

Once established these results did cast a great deal of light on the forces at work in determining the development of the terms of trade and of traded volumes.

3. The only work that, to my knowledge, consistently uses unspecified production functions when establishing the effects of growth on trade is B. Södersten (4. 1964).

An important topic of discussion in international economic policy during the 1950's and 60's has been the development of the terms of trade between industrial and less developed countries. One of the most influential schools of thought was that proposed by Raul Prebisch and a group of economists around him at the Economic Comission for Latin America.

Prebisch was averse to the thought that the Latin American economies should try to grow by increasing their exports of primary products – raw materials and food products. He feared that they then would meet falling terms of trade and that what Prebisch called "the peripheral countries" would have to export away a large share of their productivity gains to the industrial countries.

The theoretical structure of Prebisch's reasoning was intricate. The assumptions of his analysis seemed quite realistic: he took both the possibilities of collusion between firms and between labor and industry in rich countries against labor and capital in poor countries into account. The methodology behind his reasoning was, however, weak. At the bottom of his argument was a simple supply-demand model. But on to this stricture Prebisch and his colleagues at ECLA had put other theories and propositions, for instance, about the effects of business cycles on the terms of trade, about the role of monopolies and labor unions *etc.*

It was extremely difficult to see how these various propositions hang together. They were loosely fitted together and at times they seemed to be contradictory.[4]

The *ad hoc* nature of Prebisch's theorizing could be explained by the fact that trade theory had little to say about the effects of growth on trade in the early 1950's. The development of the theory of growth and trade developed in 1950's and early 1960's could be used as an Occam's razor in dealing with the earlier theories of growth and trade. It was fairly easy to see which strategic factors were at work. It was possible to derive reasonably simple and realistic hypotheses about the conditions under which a country would benefit from export-promoting policies and the conditions under which such policies might prove inefficient or even harmful.

---

4. The major sources for Prebisch's writings are United Nations Economic Commission for Latin America (written by Prebisch) (5, 1950) and R. Prebisch (2, 1959). For an evaluation and criticism of Prebisch's work see M.J. Flanders (1, 1964) and B. Södersten (4, 1964, ch. 6).

On a more general policy level, it is fair to say that the modern theory of growth and trade has been very helpful in casting light on the question of export-promoting versus import-substitution types of policies for promoting economic development. Another line of research which has treated the same general problem, but from a different angle, is the modern theory of trade policy, especially the theory of effective rates of protection. During the late 1960's and the early 1970's the question of effective rates of protection has been at the frontiers of contemporary research in trade theory.

It is however an area where established results are few and controversies many. This has to a large extent been due to the fact that difficult methodological problems are involved. At the center of the argument is the role of intermediate goods in international trade.

Empirical estimates have shown that a large share and perhaps most of international trade consists of trade in intermediate goods which are used as inputs in the production of other goods. Most of trade theory, however, has been concerned only with trade in final goods. Economists have viewed the neglect of intermediate goods in trade theory differently. Jagdish Bhagwati suggests, for instance, that it constitutes one of the central limitations of trade theory, while Murray Kemp has argued that the neglect of intermediate products in the earlier literature can be defended on the grounds that most results derived in the absence of these products are also valid in their presence.

It is an open question which of these two views is correct in connection with effective rates of protection. The essence of the notion of effective rates of protection is that it takes intermediate goods into account. We have long been aware of the fact that tariffs have a tendency to be of a cascading nature, *i.e.* the products with the highest percentage of domestic value added tend to have the highest rate of protection. It is a fact that the average level of nominal tariffs for each class tends to be an increasing function of the stage of manufacturing. However, the usefulness of the notion of the effective rate is that it is measurable. The general form of this formula for the effective rate can be written $(v'_j - v_j)/v_j$ where v'_j is the protected domestic value added and v_j is an estimated value added at free trade prices per unit in industry j. A wealth of empirical estimates of effective rates of protection have been generated using this formula.

The empirical investigations have produced results which look very interesting and promising. Small nominal tariffs have been shown to disguise large effective rates of protection. One has been left with the impression that the question of tariffs has been much more important than had earlier been realized.

At the same time that interest in these empirical estimates has been great, their validity has been questioned. The controversy has centered around two critical assumptions in the theory of effective rates of protection.

In the first place, the effective rate is derived using a partial equilibrium approach: it is assumed that the general equilibrium repercussions of tariffs are zero. Secondly, it has been assumed that intermediate factor proportions are fixed.

Both of these assumptions are far-reaching. A tariff obviously changes prices. It is then questionable if one can assume that these tariff-induced price changes will not lead to any repercussions for volumes, factor intensities *etc.* The assumption of fixed input coefficients is again not a very realistic assumption. It has been demonstrated, however, that if this assumption holds, the allocative effects of a tariff on gross output depends on the effective rate of protection.

The discussion of the role of intermediate goods in trade theory and of the meaning of effective rates of protection casts interesting light on the role of general equilibrium analysis in international economics. It is easy enough to sneer at general equilibrium analysis. At the same time, any economist taking a partial equilibrium approach will lay himself open to powerful criticism if it can be demonstrated that his results hinge on the absence of general equilibrium repercussions which are likely to exist.

In this connection, the discussions of methodology and assumptions are of a technical nature. It seems that there is a trade-off between developing a general enough abstraction of the real world on the one hand and trying to formulate and test hypotheses which are interesting on the other. So far, I am not convinced that the empirical results have not been bought at a high price in terms of the general validity of the results. The notion of the effective rate of protection still has somewhat the character of an interesting notion in search of a theory.

This does not mean that investigations of tariff structures have not proven useful. It has been shown that behind high tariff walls in, for instance, some less developed countries, industries might produce very low or even negative amounts of value added. This analysis has greatly helped to understand why policies of import-substitution have proven inefficient in many countries.

One of the most important phenomena, perhaps *the* most important, in the international economy in the post-war period is the expansion of the large international corporations. The multinational corporation is a topic of much controversy and discussion. At the risk of sounding *déjà-vu*, I will make some comments on the way international economists have treated the multinational corporation.

Economists working in the neoclassical tradition have attributed the growth of international firms among other things to their superior technology, their roles as perfectors of markets and to their capacities for overcoming artificial barriers to trade.

The distinctive feature of the international firm making direct investment in foreign countries is that it retains control of its investments. This fact can be seen from a political point of view or a more technical viewpoint. Neoclassical economists naturally take the latter course. They claim that one of the *raisons d'être* for the international firm is that it possesses superior technical knowledge and that it combines this with a high level of managerial know-how, and with possibilities of raising capital inexpensively. By making a package of complementary factors of production, it can get a higher return on each one of them than would otherwise have been possible.

In a somewhat analogous manner, the international firm can be conceived of as a perfector of markets. One can view the firm as a "privately owned market" instead of, as is standard, viewing the market as a public coordinating function open to anyone who wants to enter it as an economic agent. The big international firm can be regarded as an international market for inputs and information. It might be more efficient it is argued, to have market conditions equalized throughout the world with the help of big international firms in various branches of industry than to have the same equalization process obtained by way of international trade in goods.

The above arguments have a cheerful if not apologetic ring. It might be, for instance, that it is not competitive market conditions which are being equalized throughout the world but instead the degree of monopoly and the general conditions for monopolistic competition. Before dealing with welfare and policy aspects of direct investments I will, however, mention another line of analysis of international investments, that of Marxist economics.

There exists hardly any Marxist theory of international trade. There does, however, exist a Marxist analysis of international investments.

There have been at least two basic tenets to the Marxist theory of international investments. One has run in terms of search of new markets. Lenin (and his tutor Hobson) argued that the inner forces of capitalism, primarily the relentless pursuit and application of new innovations, force capitalists to expand to new territories to find new markets and new consumers. Thereby, argued Lenin, they will be able to postpone for a short period of time the collapse that history has in store for the capitalist system. The second tenet of Marxist theory has to do with the need for raw material. Many big firms, even the large American corporations need raw materials and sources of energy for which they have to go abroad.

The strong version of the first tenet, which argues that direct investments are necessary for the survival of the capitalist system, is not easy to uphold. Whatever one's views on capitalism might be, one should not underestimate its power for survival and even stability. This does not imply that part of international politics cannot be explained in economic terms, even in fairly crude terms like search for profits. The second tenet has, I think, to a certain extent been vindicated in recent years.

Anyone who believes that there exist depletable raw materials in short supply cannot completely disregard the Marxist line of reasoning. Nor can those who are worried about a coming energy crisis. But those who subscribe to neoclassical views one hundred per cent, who believe that substitution possibilities are endless and that shortages will never occur provided that market forces are allowed to work, can, of course, ignore Marxist views altogether.

I would like to argue that this is one of the few instances where there is something to be said in favor of the Marxist line of analysis. This is not primarily because Marxist methodology is strong. On the contrary, I think it is quite weak. But the assumptions underlying the Marxist analysis with its stress of conflict between various factors of production, of importance of power relationships and of a natural interest on the part of producers to try to limit competition and control markets seem to me more realistic than the often simple-minded, harmony-geared assumptions of neoclassical economics.

We should, however, remember that neoclassical economics is both a powerful and supple instrument of analysis. It is fully possible, by changing assumptions and emphasis of behavior rules, to see the multinational corporations as something else than a mere perfector of international markets.

One of the causes of direct investments is the desire for integration on the part of multinational firms. Large corporations wish to integrate horizontally by opening new subsidiaries in various parts of the world. This is often done in a predatory way: one or several existing, competing firms in the host country are simply bought up by a large international rival. In the process, competition is often reduced and markets are divided in an oligopolistic fashion.

Vertical integration is also a strong motive for direct investments. For instance, there are only a few companies that refine and fabricate copper. It is not astonishing that they also try to achieve control over copper mines by vertically integrating backwards in the production process. One obvious reason for vertical integration is a desire to reduce risk.

From the point of view of the international firm, both horizontal and vertical integration can have perfectly rational grounds. They might lead to better control over markets and/or more efficient ways of organizing production. This is, however, not the same as saying that they also are beneficial for governments and consumers in the host countries.

I will not try to venture into any lengthy discussion of the welfare implications of the growth of multinational firms. It is easy to point to possible positive effects for everyone involved: consumers might get better products at lower prices by the application of superior technology and factor prices might increase because of an increase in demand for labor and capital on the part of the multinational corporation.

But it is also easy to cite possible negative effects. I will mention three such effects which I think quite a few host countries have been adversely affected by. The first is that the large international firms are very creditworthy. They often raise capital for new plants or take-over bids in the local capital-market. They thereby, to the detriment of both local competitors and local industry in general, have a tendency to pre-empt this market. Secondly, they centralize expenditures on research and development to the parent country. Research in the host country is thus stifled and a brain-drain induced. Thirdly, international firms often use transfer pricing to shift taxable income, and thus taxes away from the host country and thereby affect the activities of the government of the host country negatively.

The results of an analysis of the international corporation depends to a large extent on the assumptions of the analysis. No analysis is better than the assumptions on which it rests. One of the shortcomings of traditional trade theory is that its simple-minded assumptions are ill-suited to an analysis of the growth of modern international corporations.

This does not imply, as I have already stressed, that neoclassical economics, in an up-to-date version, is incapable of dealing with multinational corporations and other recent phenomena in the international economy. On the contrary, I believe that the basic methodology of neoclassical economics is sound and can be used to deal with a great variety of economic problems. I do not believe that the neoclassical paradigm has fulfilled its historical function and will be superseded by another paradigm in the near future. The major avenue of scientific progress in economics will probably, for some time to come, be conducted within the framework of neoclassical economics. More realistic assumptions and a shift in the emphasis of the analysis will, however, probably be needed if the problems discussed here shall be dealt with in an efficient way.

It is dangerous to venture a more precise forecast about the future of international economics. I might, however, state two of my beliefs or wishes. The first has to do with market forms and possibilities of collusion. I think the prevalence of various forms of monopolistic competition and possibilities of collusion will have to be taken into account as a prerequisite for a more realistic analysis. This presupposes a renewed interest in the role of monopolistic market forms in international trade. Analysis along such lines was performed in the late 1930's and the 1940's following the work in microeconomic theory by Chamberlin and Joan Robinson. I think a revival of interest in these matters, taking into account advances in the modern theory of the firm, is long overdue.

The second has to do with a shift of emphasis in analytic problems. The old Roman question: *Cui bono*? *i.e.* for whom are certain effects beneficial should be asked more frequently. This implies, that income distribution problems, in the broad sense of the word, should be central to the analysis.

Income distribution problems were central to the classical economists. Neoclassical economists have been less concerned with them. It was not by chance that the classical economists called their science political economy. A broader approach which did not by definition exclude the political aspects of economic problems might also prove useful in dealing with some of the pertinent problems of the 1970's. Generalization as well as specialization is one of the elements of scientific progress.

World trade has grown exceptionally fast in the post-war period. The forces behind the internationalization process have been strong. Technical progress in transport and communication has played an important role. Increased returns to scale in production and high income elasticities for differentiated products have also had their impact. These and many other factors have favored international specialization and trade. The forces working for economic interdependence among nations seem irresistable.

At the same time, we should not forget that the national state is still in the 1970's the dominant entity. On the other hand there are also counterfactors at work. For instance, the international repercussions on various national economies are less than they used to be. Most countries, notably those in Western Europe, have not been so highly affected by international business cycle fluctuations as they were in the inter-war period. Labor-markets, especially those in Western Europe, have been influenced by regional migration, but we have not witnessed any migrations on the scale of those which took place in the nineteenth century from Europe to the United States.

It is therefore an open question if the degree of interdependence is increasing or not. There are undoubtedly many economists who would argue that the forces behind the internationalization process are strongest and that the national state will wither away. I am not convinced that this will be the case. The forces working for a national identity – perhaps a new type of identity, be it from dominating neighbours or a new type of changed social and political system – are also strong in many countries. Whether existing trends toward internationalization or new forms of nationalism will get the upper hand is impossible to say. This is primarily a political question.

In order to deal with these and other contemporary problems it is necessary to taken a broad view and not assume away factors which might prove central to the analysis. Economic theory is both a supple and powerful tool of analysis. We should not let a misguided scientific puritanism lure us away from dealing with important problems. In order to deal with the problems of the 20th century we can no longer continue with assumptions applicable to the 19th century.

References

1. Flanders, M.J., "Prebisch and Protectionism: An Evaluation," *Economic Journal*, LXXIV (1964).
2. Prebisch, R., "Commercial Policy in the Underdeveloped Countries," *American Economic Review, Papers and Proceedings*, IL (1959).
3. Robinson, J., "The Need for a Reconsideration of the Theory of International Trade," in M.B. Connolly and A.K. Swoboda, *International Trade and Money*, London, 1973.
4. Södersten, B., *A Study of Economic Growth and International Trade*, Stockholm, 1964.
5. United Nations Economic Commission for Latin America, *The Economic Development of Latin America and its Principal Problems*, New York, 1950.

Final observations

Frits J. de Jong

Mr. Chairman, I must say that I am afraid that you are a little over-optimistic, because if I am supposed to give a story in which each element is given its proper accent and its proper weight, I should present a piece in the form of a well-balanced composition. Unfortunately, I am not able to do so, because the number of subjects and topics touched upon is so overwhelmingly large. Moreover, one cannot really prepare a lecture like this, because one has to sit down and wait for what will be said by the various speakers. It is only due to the fact that a team of Assistant Professors has very rapidly and precisely provided me with notes on what has been said during these days, that I can venture to undertake the task of making some concluding remarks. What I am going to present to you, then, is a kind of rhapsody, and not a really solid composition. The only thing I may trust is that it will not turn out to be a *Rhapsody in Blue*, to quote the expression used by Negro singers, in which "blue" means pessimistic or gloomy.

Let me start with the last lecture we have had the pleasure of hearing here, that is the one given by Professor Södersten from Göteborg. I propose to do so for two reasons. First of all, because this lecture is still fresh in our minds, since it was given this morning, and secondly, because Södersten has exactly done what he had been asked to do. He has really given a survey of what he believes to have been the most important points in the development of International Economics during the past 25 years, after which he has outlined his views with respect to what may be expected to happen in the same field during the years to come.

I will not try to summarize his lecture, and neither do I wish to summarize the other lectures. Let me only touch upon some special points. What struck me most is that Professor Södersten emphasized the idea that what is really necessary is a combination of pure theory or systematic thinking, and empirical investigation. This may sound as

forcing an open door, but, indeed, it needs to be said and emphasized
again and again, because – and here my rhapsody does become
somewhat blue – we see today that there are people who do a lot of
theorizing but who do not cary very much about actual facts, whereas,
on the other hand, there are the "empiricists", who do a lot of statistical
investigation but who do not care very much about the underlying
theory. Both parties are wrong. The empiricists are wrong because they
overlook the fact that they always run the risk that their correlations will
turn out to be nonsense-correlations. So what we really need is a theory
to show why a correlation we have found is not just a correlation by mere
chance, but why it must be *expected* to be a correlation.

Moreover, it is sometimes forgotten that it is impossible to collect facts
without starting from a theory. That is a point Walter Eucken already
made in 1939. He pointed out that, in order to be able to collect data, you
must make a choice. In order to be able to make this choice you must
have a point of view, and in order to have a point of view, you must have
a theory. Now, the initial theory may be very simple: it may be the kind
of theory as stored in everyday language or common sense. But it is a
theory nevertheless. And then, by playing ideas backward and forward
between thinking and observation of facts, we may succeed in
developing a more sophisticated theory which in the course of time may
approach reality more and more closely without, however, reaching it
completely, because human mind is too limited to be able to comprise the
whole of reality. Moreover, our models would become much too
complicated to be manageable. Theory, then, is always a kind of
approximation, and it will always remain "abstract" to a certain degree.
The criterion for distinguishing "good" theory from "bad" theory is not
only that good theory is acceptable from the viewpoint of logic but also
that it can be used for the practical purpose of making forecasts.

This is why I am so glad that Professor Södersten has stressed the
point that we should be in search of theory, or, as he has put it, of
"equilibrium theory." Now, this expression is all right with me, provided
we take it in a very broad sense, that is, if we accept the idea that
"equilibrium theory" in a broad sense consists of two parts: first,
equilibrium theory in a narrow sense which demonstrates the tendencies
existing in economic life that push the system into a situation of
equilibrium, and secondly, the anti-equilibrium theory which shows the
forces that drive the economic system away from an equilibrium
position.

A second point that struck me in Södersten's lecture was the search for market forms. Small wonder that I was struck by this because my doctoral thesis was on that subject-matter. Market forms have been largely neglected in economic theory, so it was important that Professor Södersten discussed them during his exposition of the problem of multinational firms. He and I strive after the same purpose. In September 1972 an international colloquium on the growth of the large multinational corporation was held in Rennes, Bretagne. I submitted a paper on multinational enterprises and the market form. I was somewhat disappointed to see that, while an important mass of empirical evidence with respect to concentration ratios, *etc.*, was produced by the visitors to the congress, some of these were jumping from this evidence to conclusions concerning the degree of competition. This is a very dangerous procedure: empirical evidence of concentration ratios by itself does not mean very much if it is not backed by some kind of theory, or at least by a consistent classification of market forms.[1]

This leads me to another point with respect to this congress. It is remarkable that nothing whatsoever has been said about the theory of oligopoly, which, in a sense, is a blank in our body of economic theory. This is indeed a lacuna. It would have been important to have had an exposition on the theory of heterogeneous oligopoly, because this is the most important market form in the real world. We all know that there are many books and articles on oligopoly, but the difficulty is that they are not practically relevant. I suggest that this would be a fine topic for our next congress, say 25 years hence.

Professor Södersten has touched upon the Marxist line of analysis with its stress on conflicts between various factors of production, on the importance of relative power, and on the interest on the part of producers to try to limit competition and to control markets. According to Södersten, this seems to be a more realistic approach than the often simple-minded harmony-geared assumptions of neo-classical economics. This may be very true, and I think that the mutual influence of western and Marxist thought has been too weak in the past. It may be true that the methodology of Marxist economics is sometimes weak; nevertheless, I think that in the same way as the Sovjets nowadays import more and more of western economics, we might well have a closer look at

1. F.J. de Jong (5, 1973). Unfortunately, this paper contains quite a few errors of print. A sheet of errata may be obtained from the author on request.

Marxist economics, and see what is going on there. I am not necessarily saying that we should take over everything they have stated: we ought to remain critical, not only with respect to Marxist theory, of course, but also with respect to our own theory.

It has been suggested that it is possible to subscribe to the basically sound methodological ideas of neo-classical economics without accepting its debatable simple-minded assumptions. This contra-distinction is not entirely clear to me, because there may well be a connection between assumptions made and method adopted. May we be sure that the methodology of neo-classical theory is always sound? Perhaps we may agree that it is sound enough for most purposes of the theory of international trade. Or may we not? Next time, 25 years hence, it would be important to have an exposition on the question of what is really the interdependence between assumptions made and methods adopted. I would agree with Professor Kaldor's idea that the entrepreneurs' preference for certain forms of monopolistic competition and possibilities of collusion will have to be taken into account, and that problems of income distribution in the broad sense of the word will essentially remain the same in the near future as they are now, but that the neo-classical method of analysis will not give us the solution of these problems.

Like any complete economic theory, the theory of international economic relations is a synthesis of two things: a theory of the real sector of the economy and a theory of the monetary sector. The workshop of economic science may be compared to a "production column," that is, the system of successive stages of production, from the raising of the primordial products from the soil to the retail trade. Any stage of the production column sells its products to the next stage. Analogously, we may call the price theorist's workshop a "stage of the production column of economic science": it "sells" its "products" to the theory of international trade. The system of market forms is a component part of this "product."

Another component is the theory of consumer demand. It is, therefore, important that Professor Barten of Louvain has presented a summary of the trends in the analysis of consumer demand. In this context, Professor Barten has been talking about the paradigm of the theory of the consumer. I have always been puzzled by the word "paradigm" and the way it is used in present-day economics. According to the *Concise Oxford Dictionary,* a "paradigm" is an example or a pattern, especially of inflection of the noun or the verb. What, then, does it mean in economics? It would have to be a kind of example or a pattern, especially of the analysis of an economic system. If this is correct, you could call a theory a "paradigm" in the special case that you have a certain prescientific outlook on the world and then try to devise a theory for that world.

Let me say a few words about this point. It is very much in vogue today to state that theories are really inspired by ideologies. This is the Marxist point of view. I feel that, as a *general* statement, it is sheer nonsense. But in some special cases there is something to it. It may be that you have a very optimistic outlook on the world, in the sense that you feel intuitively (or that you *want* to feel) that very strong equilibrium tendencies prevail in the real world. In America we hear many people say that the "hard, competitive system," which is the American way of life, is the best way of life that could ever exist in this world. If you do believe this, it is only a matter of course that you are tempted to devise economic theories that describe such a world. And that is what neoclassical authors do. If, on the other hand, you do not believe this, that is if you believe that there have always been clashes between two classes of people, then you try to devise a Marxist theory.

This point of view is all right with me when we deal with the starting point of theory, because one has to start with *something* that is in one's mind: common speech, common sense, and the ideology implied in it; but it is very dangerous to stick to it. What ought to be done, is to devise a theory and then to test both its assumptions and its results empirically.

Some people do not care very much about testing. They seem to think: "If my theory does not fit in with the facts, so much the worse for the facts". This, in fact, was the point made by Professor Cramer, who interruptively said that you have to be very careful about all this: either you like to test, or you do not. But *if* you like to test, you have to assume that your data are reliable. If, then, your theory turns out to be contrary to observed facts, you have to refute the theory, whatever the ideology may have been that was underlying it in its initial stage. An ideology cannot save a theory that is refuted by empirical testing.

Talking about utility, Professor Barten gave a nice circumscription of the utility function. He said: utility is simply a name for the idea that bundles of goods can be ordered. A bundle preferred to another bundle will be given a higher rank-number. What we as economists do, is that we choose a set of actions with respect to the ordering of preferences as our point of departure, and in this analysis only price-goods (including

services) are relevant. It is assumed that for at least one of these goods
the consumer can never reach a situation of oversaturation, and there are
some more special assumptions. His point is, I think, that – apart from
theoretical reflections in which, for instance, he gave a very interesting
parallel to production functions – the crucial question is whether or not
these preferences are to be taken as data for economic theory.

This is a very important point indeed. Some people seem to believe
that data are forever fixed in the framework of no matter what kind of
economic theory. This, again, is sheer nonsense, and I am glad that
Professor Barten stressed this point. If you look at different kinds of
economic theory, you will find that the set of data is different for each of
them. In Paretian theory, for instance, data are different from those in
Keynesian theory.

But, still more important, one should always be aware of the
possibility that the day may come on which something that one has
accepted as a datum turns out to be an endogenous variable in another
model. That may well be so with consumer's preferences as they are
described in the Paretian general equilibrium system. This means that
you have to ask yourself whether preferences can be changed by man's
own free choice – one of the points Professor Barten mentioned
explicitly – or by social control, or by influences exerted by society, or
also by producers making advertisements, or by the government. This is
a very important problem, and it is certainly worth-while investigating it.
The practical purport of such an investigation is mainly that we want to
know how producers and the government can influence consumers'
preferences, because if they can and they know they can, then two things
may follow in practice. First, if the government should happen to believe
that it is desirable to diminish the number of cars on the roads, it will
have to know how to change consumers' preferences in such a way as to
let them desire less cars. Secondly, I would like to add another point, one
which has not been touched upon in this conference, perhaps because it
is less clear. Cannot we try to expand the idea of utility function to the
field of the entrepreneur? Simple textbooks state that entrepreneurial
behaviour is completely governed by profit maximization. That is all
right for a first or second year textbook, but we do know that the real
world is not like that. I am not saying that profits do not matter. My
impression is that profits do matter, but that they are not the only motive
of entrepreneurial behaviour. Entrepreneurs are certainly motivated by
more things than just profit. Could not we try to devise a kind of utility

function in the entrepreneur's mind the arguments of which would be profit, market share, continuity of the firm, social prestige, power, quietness of life? Hicks once said that the best of all monopoly profits is a quiet life.[2]

The difficulty about all this is, of course, that I am now running counter to Barten's correct statement that the arguments in utility functions must be measurable, at least theoretically – that is, that they must be quantities, because quantities are measurable by definition – and that they must have a price. For instance, how do we measure power? By Lerner's degree of monopoly? And how do we measure its price? One may answer that, commonly speaking, power does not have a price, because it is not a market-good. But is this argument valid? Let us re-read Wicksteed, who wrote that "price" in the narrower sense of "the money for which a material thing, a service, or a privilege can be obtained," is simply a special case of "price" on the wider sense of "the terms on which alternatives are offered to us."[3] Now, if an entrepreneur wants to enlarge his power, he has to sacrifice something. Question: *what* does he have to sacrifice, and how can we measure it in terms of money? If we could arrive at developing a measuring-rod for power and at the same time define its "price" in a measurable way, we could include power in the arguments of the utility function.

True, all this is somewhat hazy: I am only stating a problem without offering its solution. One may, therefore, suggest an alternative way of tackling the analysis of entrepreneurial behaviour: one may try to reason along the lines of the behavioural scientists, as Nentjes has suggested,[4] and I feel much sympathy for this idea. On the other hand, it must be conceded that the behavioural theory of the firm, taken as a theory of price, is still in its infancy: it has not yet been elaborated in such a way as to produce a general equilibrium system of oligopolistic markets. Here by "equilibrium system" is again meant equilibrium system in its broad sense in which it comprises equilibrium theory in the narrow sense as well as theories of anti-equilibrium. I am saying all this, because I believe that a commentator's primary task is not to summarize the speakers but to give an outlook on further problems. Here is another subject for a future symposium.

2. J. R. Hicks (3, 1953, p. 369).
3. Ph. H. Wicksteed (11, 1946, p. 28).
4. A. Nentjes (9, 1971).

Let us now turn to the field of macro-economics, and more specifically to the lecture given by Professor Kaldor of Cambridge, who said that his ideas have been undergoing a constant change. We should not have expected otherwise, because, if one's ideas do not change any more, one is ready for retirement. Professor Kaldor said that in his original growth models he had tried to demonstrate that the growth path of an economy would be Harrod's natural growth path. This is the growth path as determined by exogenous factors: resources and human knowledge whereby "resources" is meant capital accumulation and the rate of growth of the labour force. What is his present view? If I have followed him correctly, I should say that his main endeavour was to state two things. First, that some people seem to have forgotten that investments do not only have an income effect, but also a capacity effect, which means that the production frontier will shift to the north-east as a consequence of investments. The old classical content was that this frontier will not shift at the same rate as the capital accumulation. This process will bring the economy to a point where the rate of capital accumulation will govern and limit the growth of the economy. Now, this is exactly the point Kaldor wanted to reject. He said that it is not true because you can decide how much of the national product you are going to invest and how much you are going to consume. Neither can the labour force limit the national production, because there is always disguised unemployment in agriculture. In the course of industrialization we see a reduction of the labour force in agriculture accompanied by an increase in the absolute production in this sector. This means that agricultural productivity as measured in kilogrammes per hectare is increasing. This may well be true for a rather long period, but will it be true forever? I can hardly believe so, because the point will eventually be reached at which the outflow of labour will come to a standstill. Let us assume for a moment that Kaldor is right in stating it is possible to achieve the entire agricultural production with, say, two percent of the world population. If the process does go on in the way as outlined by Kaldor, it will come to a standstill at the very moment that only two percent of the population is still working in agriculture, and then the conclusion that the growth of the population is one of the forces limiting the growth of agricultural production will become true again. So, I do not think that I could accept Kaldor's view as a generally valid theory, although there may be something to it in not too long a period.

Kaldor's second point was the view he now holds about complementarity of factors of production. Here again my position would be less strong than his. I would certainly be prepared to agree that substitution has been stressed too much in current literature, and that the importance of complementarity has been underestimated. Let me only recall the production function as devised by Simon Kuipers, who stressed exactly this point, though we should not exaggerate.[5] It does not seem to be realistic to believe that complementarity is the only possibility: a certain limited degree of substitutability does exist. Indeed, Kaldor himself stated that when certain kinds of energy are more or less exhausted, human mind will find substitutes. How could one be able to find substitutes in a world where only complementary is said to occur?

There is, none the less, something to Kaldor's point of view. This is his idea that primary production is one of the limiting factors, because secondary and even tertiary production feed on the products of the primary sector. Here he has got a point. It is also one of the ideas underlying the Report of the Club of Rome, and it is good to stress it once more. Let us hope that in not too remote a future Professor Kaldor will write an exposition more elaborate than he was able to give us here, because time was too short for him to make his ideas completely explicit.

Finally, I come to the lecture presented by my friend Jan Pen. He and I have at least one thing in common: both of us have our hobbies. One of Professor Pen's hobbies as reformulated in my terminology, is to state that monetary theory is about the same thing as *monetarist* theory. But this is not so. "Monetary" theory is the theory about a sector of the economy that happens to exist, namely, the monetary sector. Some people ask "Does money matter?", and the answer will be: "Of course it does!" Why indeed should we have a banking system guided by a central bank, if money would not matter? We had better ask then, whether it matters in the same way as the "monetarists" look at it. The "monetarist" view is that money does not only matter, but that the monetary sector decisively determines the economy's woe and weal. Although I am convinced that "monetary" theory is an important branch

---

5. As a simple formula satisfying his diagrams 3.2.1 and 3.2.2., he presented in his mimeographed doctoral thesis on the same subject matter:

$$X = a_1 N - a_2 \frac{N^2}{K} - a_3 K$$

with $a_1, a_2, a_3 > 0$ and $a_1^2 - 4a_2 a_3 > 0$, where X denotes the national product, N the input of labour, and K the real capital stock. This production equation was tested empirically. The parameters a represent the state of arts. S. K. Kuipers (8, 1973, pp. 561-571).

of economics, I have always rejected the "monetarist" view: the latter exaggerates the importance of the monetary sector.

Pen seems to have fallen a victim to the misunderstanding that all monetary theory presented during the last few decades is in essence "monetarist" theory, but this is simply not so. Let me elucidate this by means of two examples.

First, consider Keynes' *General Theory*. It cannot be denied that Keynes presented a theory of money – a "monetary" theory – but he was certainly not a "monetarist": he did believe that money matters, but we all know that he would never have subscribed to the view that it is monetary developments that, in the last instance, determine the developments in the real sector (which is the "monetarist" view). Keynes expected more good to be gained by pursuing a policy of sustaining effective demand than by following a monetary policy, although he did not deny that the latter can support the former. (What he neglected was the influence of the balance of payments, and here lies his main shortcoming.) Pen seems to be too much influenced by those "Keynesians" who lay all stress on Keynes' theory of effective demand but neglect the fact that the Keynesian model does contain a monetary sector, which is by no means unimportant.

Secondly, we have the case of Dutch monetary theory, more specifically, the little monetary model developed by Dr. M. W. Holtrop, the former President of the Netherlands Bank.[6] Some people, including Pen, believe that Holtrop is a monetarist. I have denied this in my reflection of Holtrop's theory, which has been read by Holtrop, and he did not oppose my view.[7] The appearance of Holtrop being a monetarist is created by the fact that Holtrop's theory assigns a central place in the management of the economy to monetary policy as reflected specifically in changes over time in the mass of liquidity, much in the same way as the American monetarist school does. But one should not lose sight of the fact that Holtrop was a central banker, whose appointed task it is "to regulate the value of the Netherlands monetary unit in such a way as is deemed most conducive to the welfare of the country, and therewith to stabilize that value as far as possible: ... to provide for the monetary

6. See on this: F.J. de Jong (6, 1973, ch. 4).
7. For instance, where Holtrop's theory is characterized as a kind of neo-quantity theory with a Keynesian flavour, springing from the root of J.G. Koopmans' 1933 analysis of the conditions of monetary equilibrium (which, in its turn, goes back to Hayek and Wicksell). F.J. de Jong (6, 1973, pp. 2-3).

circulation in the Netherlands as far as this circulation consists of bank notes; ... and to exercise supervision over the credit system."[8] It was, then, quite natural for him to emphasize changes in the demand for and supply of liquidity as strategic factors explaining developments in the economy – but this does not mean that Holtrop believes that these developments are caused by monetary factors *alone*. Holtrop too, went through the mill of Keynesian theory, and he knows that the motivations of the economic behaviour of the public depend largely upon what is going on in the real sector, and that fiscal policy is also an important instrument of economic policy. The latter policy has, of course, its monetary consequences, but its main concern is the regulation of effective demand. Holtrop may well be somewhat more monetary-minded than Keynes, but he is certainly not a Friedman-style "monetarist."

Professor Pen has also dealt with the contrast between Keynesian and neo-classical macro-economics as theories relating to the real sector. He has certainly got a point in saying that the essence of the contrast is *not* to be found in the wide-spread belief that prices are supposed to be rigid in Keynes' theory whereas they are considered flexible in neo-classical theory. True, prices are flexible in neoclassical theory and rigid in "Keynesian theory" (as distinct from "Keynes' theory": there is a difference between Keynes and the Keynesians). It is also true that Keynes observed that wages are rigid in the real world (at least into the downward direction). But on pp. 259-267 of the *General Theory* he gave an analysis of what would happen if wages and prices were *not* rigid, and he concluded that, generally speaking, wage cuts, accompanied by a reduction of prices (p. 262), will not automatically restore full employment.[9] So, Keynes did introduce wage and price flexibility into his system, and complete mathematical models of Keynes' theory as devised by his commentators contain the price level as a variable. The "Keynesians" have overlooked this, problably because they have been focusing too much on the model of the real sector of the Keynesian system, which can be represented graphically by the famous 45°-diagram.[10] In this truncated model the price level is indeed a predetermined

8. Article of Bank Act 1948 (1).
9. This was already pointed out by L.R. Klein (7, 1947, pp. 88-90) and D. Dillard (2, 1948, p. 25).
10. This may also be one of the reasons why the older Keynesians believed that money would not matter.

variable which may be taken as a constant quantity – but it does not describe the *complete* Keynesian system.

What, then, is really the difference between Keynesian and neo-classical macro-economics? Keynesian theory is essentially a demand theory, although the supply side of the system is certainly neither lacking in Keynes' own system,[11] nor in the post-Keynesian theories. But the supply side does not become much more than a shadow in the work of neo-Keynesian economists who refuse to use the concept of a macro-economic production function in their theories of growth.[12] Neo-classical models, on the other hand, are one-sided supply models: the demand side is here brushed from the table by simply *assuming* that savings will *always* equal investments ($S = I$, where both S and I are taken as *ex ante* quantities). We may label this assumption "Say's Law"; it may be called "Say's Law in a wider sense" if it is assumed that monetary policy will always succeed in keeping S equal to I.

Professor Pen made an important point when he suggested that the three types of macro-economic theory – monetary, Keynesian, and classical – ought to be brought to a synthesis. This is exactly the project we are working on in the Macro-Economics Section of our Department of Economics. Dr. Kuipers' Ph.D. thesis on *A Demand and Supply Model of Economic Growth* (already quoted) is an attempt to make a synthesis of Keynesian and classical growth theories (in so far as these theories are not mutually inconsistent). Mr. B.S. Wilpstra is now preparing a Ph.D. thesis presenting a model in which the monetary sector is integrated into Kuipers' model. The next step will be to elaborate this theory into a model for an open economy with a public sector. Finally, this model should be made operational and tested statistically. This is a long way to go, but it seems to me that it is the only promising way leading to the goal of an operationally meaningful growth

11. That Keynes' theory was just a demand theory without a solid supply side was suggested by D. Patinkin (10, 1949). His view was contested by F.J. de Jong (4, 1954).
12. We must agree with Mrs. Joan Robinson that many awkward things can be said about the concept of a macro-economic production function. How do you measure the capital stock in a way that is satisfactory from a theoretical point of view, and how do you solve the problem of aggregating a large number of micro-economic production functions into one macro-economic relation? These are unsolved problems. But I am afraid that we cannot really do without a production function in our macro-economic growth theory, however questionable such a function might be. It seems that Professor Kaldor now holds the same view, considering the concept of "production frontier" he has used in his lecture.

theory that makes sense from a theoretical point of view and is practically useful at the same time. And this is how theory ought to be.

Mr. Chairman, I hope that you will agree that my Rhapsody has not been Blue. The lectures presented have been very instructive and we shall remember them for a long time.

References

1. Bank's Annual Report for 1948 (English), pp. 69-77.
2. Dillard, D., *The Economics of John Maynard Keynes,* New York, 1948.
3. Hicks, J.R., "Annual Survey of Economic Theory: The Theory of Monopoly," *Econometrica,* III (1935), pp. 1-20. Reprinted in *Readings in Price Theory,* Philadelphia, Toronto and London, 1953, pp. 361-383.
4. Jong, F.J. de, "Supply Functions in Keynesian Economics," *Economic Journal,* LXIV (1954), pp. 3-24.
5. Jong, F.J. de, "Multinational Enterprises and the Market Form," in *The Growth of the Large Multinational Corporation,* Centre national de la recherche scientifique, Paris, 1973, pp. 133-179.
6. Jong, F.J. de, *Developments of Monetary Theory in the Netherlands,* Rotterdam, 1973.
7. Klein, L.R., *The Keynesian Revolution,* New York, 1947.
8. Kuipers, S.K., "A Demand and Supply Model of Economic Growth," *De Economist,* CXXI (1973), pp. 553-608.
9. Nentjes, A., "Marginalisme en behaviourisme in de theorie van de onderneming," *Economisch-Statische Berichten,* LVI (1971), pp. 1052-1054.
10. Patinkin, D., "Involuntary Unemployment and the Keynesian Supply Function," *Economic Journal,* LIX (1949), pp. 360-383.
11. Wicksteed, Ph.H., *The Common Sense of Political Economy,* Volume I, Revised Edition, London, 1946.

PART II

From substantive to procedural rationality

Herbert A. Simon

Rational human behavior has been a central object of study in the two distinct disciplines of economics and cognitive psychology. A person unfamiliar with the histories and contemporary research preoccupations of these two disciplines might imagine that there were close relations between them – a constant flow of theoretical concepts and empirical findings from the one to the other and back. In actual fact, communication has been quite infrequent. In the United States, at least, there seem to be no doctoral programs in economics that require their students to master the psychological literature of rational choice, and no psychology programs that insist that their students become acquainted with economic theories of rationality. (I would be gratified to learn that such programs exist, but if they do, they are inconspicuous in the extreme.)

This state of mutual ignorance (perhaps *noblesse oblige* is the right term for it) has a simple explanation. The single term, "rationality," has had an essentially different meaning in economics from its meaning in cognitive psychology. Traditionally, economists have been interested mostly in what I call "substantive rationality," while cognitive psychologists have been interested in a quite distinct concept which I shall call "procedural rationality."

My intent in this paper is, first, to explain the two terms "substantive rationality" and "procedural rationality" – the difference between them, and their relations as well. I shall try to document the fact that during the past 25 years economists have begun to show growing interest in procedural rationality, and to give reasons for believing that procedural rationality will become one of the central concerns of economics over the next 25 years.

Substantive Rationality

Behavior is substantively rational when it is appropriate to the achievement of given goals within the limits imposed by given conditions and constraints.[1] Notice that, by this definition, the rationality of behavior depends upon the actor in only a single respect – his goals. Given these goals, the rational behavior is determined entirely by the characteristics of the environment in which it takes place.

Suppose, for example, that the problem is to minimize the cost of a nutritionally adequate diet, where nutritional adequacy is defined in terms of lower bounds on intakes of certain proteins, vitamins, and minerals, and upper and lower bounds on calories, and where the unit prices and compositions of the obtainable foods are specified. This diet problem can be (and has been) formulated as a straightforward linear-programming problem, and the correct solution found by applying the simplex algorithm or some other computational procedure. Given the goal of minimizing cost and the definition of "nutritionally adequate," there are no two ways about it – there is only one substantively rational solution.

Classical economic analysis rests on two fundamental assumptions. The first assumption is that the economic actor has a particular goal – e.g., utility maximization or profit maximization. The second assumption is that the economic actor is substantively rational. Given these two assumptions, and given a description of a particular economic environment, economic analysis (descriptive or normative) could usually be carried out using such standard tools as the differential calculus, linear programming, or dynamic programming.

Thus, the assumptions of utility or profit maximization, on the one hand, and the assumption of substantive rationality, on the other, freed economics from any dependence upon psychology. As long as these assumptions went unchallenged, there was no reason why an economist should acquaint himself with the psychological literature on human cognitive processes or human choice. There was absolutely no point at which the findings of psychological research could be injected into the process of economic analysis. The irrelevance of psychology to economics was complete.

---

1. *Cf.* the entry under "rationality" in J. Gould and W.L. Kolb (9, 1964, pp. 573-574).

Procedural Rationality

Behavior is procedurally rational when it is the outcome of appropriate deliberation. Its procedural rationality depends on the process that generated it. When psychologists use the term "rational," it is usually procedural rationality they have in mind. William James,[2] for example, uses "rationality" as synonymous with "the peculiar thinking process called reasoning." Conversely, behavior tends to be described as "irrational" in psychology when it represents impulsive response to affective mechanisms without an adequate intervention of thought.

Perhaps because "rationality" resembles "rationalism" too closely, and because psychology's primary concern is with process rather than outcome, psychologists tend to use phrases like "cognitive processes" and "intellective processes" when they write about rationality in behavior. This shift in terminology may have contributed further to the mutual isolation of the concepts of substantive and procedural rationality.

The Study of Cognitive Processes

The process of rational calculation is only interesting when it is non-trivial – that is, when the substantively rational response to a situation is not instantly obvious. If you put a quarter and a dime before a subject and tell him that he may have either one, but not both, it is easy to predict which he will choose, but not easy to learn anything about his cognitive processes. Hence, procedural rationality is usually studied in problem situations – situations in which the subject must gather information of various kinds and process it in different ways in order to arrive at a reasonable course of action, a solution to the problem.

Historically, there have been three main categories of psychological research on cognitive processes: learning, problem solving, and concept attainment. Learning research is concerned with the ways in which information is extracted from one problem situation and stored in such a way as to facilitate the solving of similar problems subsequently. Problem solving research (in this narrower sense) focusses especially upon the complementary roles of trial-and-error procedures and insight

2. W. James (12, 1890, ch. 22).

in reaching problem solutions. Concept attainment research is concerned
with the ways in which rules of generalizations are extracted from a
sequence of situations and used to predict subsequent situations. Only in
recent years, particularly since the Second World War, has there been
much unification of theory emerging from these three broad lines of
research.

Computational Efficiency

Let us return for a moment to the optimal diet problem which we used to
illustrate the concept of substantive rationality. From a procedural
standpoint, our interest would lie not in the problem solution – the
prescribed diet itself – but in the method used to discover it. At first
blush, this appears to be more a problem in the computational
mathematics than in psychology. But that appearance is deceptive.

What is the task of computational mathematics? It is to discover the
relative efficiencies of different computational processes for solving
problems of various kinds. Underlying any question of computational
efficiency is a set of assumptions about the capabilities of the computing
system. For an omniscient being, there are no questions of computational efficiency, because the consequences of any tautology are known as
soon as the premises are stated; and computation is simply the spinning
out of such consequences.[3]

Nowadays, when we are concerned with computational efficiency, we
are concerned with the computing time or effort that would be required
to solve a problem by a system, basically serial in operation, requiring
certain irreducible times to perform an addition, a multiplication, and a
few other primitive operations. To compare the simplex method with
some other method for solving linear programming problems, we seek to
determine how much total computing time each method would need.

The search for computational efficiency is a search for procedural
rationality, and computational mathematics is a normative theory of such
rationality. In this normative theory, there is no point in prescribing a
particular substantively rational solution if there exists no procedure for
finding that solution with an acceptable amount of computing effort. So,

3. This statement is a little oversimple in ignoring the distinction between induction and
deduction, but greater precision is not needed for our purposes.

for example, although there exist optimal (substantively rational) solutions for combinatorial problems of the travelling-salesman type, and although these solutions can be discovered by a finite enumeration of alternatives, actual computation of the optimum is infeasible for problems of any size and complexity. The combinatorial explosion of such problems simply outraces the capacities of computers, present and prospective.

Hence, a theory of rationality for problems like the travelling-salesman problem is not a theory of best solutions – of substantive rationality – but a theory of efficient computational procedures to find good solutions – a theory of procedural rationality. Notice that this change in viewpoint involves not only a shift from the substantive to the procedural, but a shift also from concern for optimal solutions to a concern for good solutions. I shall discuss this point later.

Computation: Risky Decisions

But now it is time to return to psychology and its concern with computational efficiency. Man, viewed as a thinker, is a system for processing information. What are his procedures for rational choice?

One method of testing a theory of human rational choice is to study choice behavior in relatively simple and well-structured laboratory situations where the theory makes specific predictions about how subjects will behave. This method has been used by a number of investigators – including W. Edwards, G. Pitts, A. Rapaport, and A. Tversky – to test whether human decisions in the face of uncertainty and risk can be explained by the normative concepts of statistical decision theory. This question is particularly interesting because these norms are closely allied, both historically and logically, to the notions of substantive rationality that have prevailed in economics, and make no concessions to computational difficulties – they never choose the computable second-best over the non-computable best.

Time does not permit me to review this extensive literature that this line of inquiry has produced. A recent review by Rapaport[4] covers experimental tests of SEU (subjective expected utility) maximization, of Bayesian strategies for sequential decisions, and of other models of

4. A. Rapaport and T.S. Wallsten (17, 1972).

rational choice under uncertainty. I think the evidence can be fairly summarized by the statements (a) that it is possible to construct gambles sufficiently simple and transparent that most subjects will respond to them in a manner consistent with SEU theory; but (b) the smallest departures from this simplicity and transparency produce behavior in many or most subjects that *cannot* be explained by SEU or Bayesian models. I will illustrate this statement by just three examples, which I hope are not atypical.

The first is the phenomenon of event matching.[5] Suppose that you present a subject with a random sequence of X's and O's, of which 70% are X's and 30% O's. You ask the subject to predict the next symbol, rewarding him for the number of correct predictions. "Obviously" the rational behavior is always to predict X. This is what subjects almost never do.[6] Instead, they act as though the sequence were patterned, not random, and guess by trying to extrapolate the pattern. This kind of guessing will lead X to be guessed in proportion to the frequency with which it occurs in the sequence. As a result, the sequence of guesses has about the same statistical properties as the original sequence, but the prediction accuracy is lower than if X had been predicted each time (58% instead of 70%).

In a recent study by Kahneman & Tversky,[7] a quite different phenomenon showed up. The rational procedure for combining new information with old is Bayes' Theorem. If a set of probabilities has been assigned to the possible outcomes of an uncertain event, a new evidence is presented, Bayes' Theorem provides an algorithm for revising the prior probabilities to take the new evidence into account. One obvious consequence of Bayes' Theorem is that the more extensive and reliable the new evidence, the greater should be its influence on the new probabilities. Another consequence is that the new probabilities should not depend on the new evidence only, but upon the prior probabilities as well. In the experiments conducted by Kahneman and Tversky, the estimates of subjects were independent of the reliability of the new evidence, and did not appear to be influenced by the prior probabilities at all.

---

5. J. Feldman (7, 1963).
6. The sole exceptions of which I am aware of are well-known and expert game theorists who served as subjects in this experiment at the Rand Corporation many years ago!
7. D. Kahneman and A. Tversky (14, 1973).

On the other hand, Ward Edwards[8] has reviewed a large body of experimental evidence describing quite conservative behavior. In these experiments, subjects did not revise prior probability estimates nearly as much as would be called for by Bayes' Theorem. It appears, then that humans can either overrespond to new evidence or ignore it, depending upon the precise experimental circumstances. If these differences in behavior manifest themselves even in laboratory situations so simple that it would be possible for subjects to carry out the actual Bayes calculations, we should be prepared to find variety at least as great when people are required to face the complexities of the real world.

Man's Computational Efficiency

If these laboratory demonstrations of human failure to follow the canons of substantive rationality in choice under uncertainty caused any surprise to economists (and I don't know that they did), they certainly did not to experimental psychologists familiar with human information processing capabilities.

Like a modern digital computer's, Man's equipment for thinking is basically serial in organization. That is to say, one step in thought follows another, and solving a problem requires the execution of a large number of steps in sequence. The speed of his elementary processes,.especially arithmetic processes, is much slower, of course, than those of a computer, but there is much reason to think that the basic repertoire of processes in the two systems is quite similar.[9] Man and computer can both recognize symbols (patterns), store symbols, copy symbols, compare symbols for identity, and output symbols. These processes seem to be the fundamental components of thinking as they are of computation.

For most problems that Man encounters in the real world, no procedure that he can carry out with his information processing equipment will enable him to discover the optimal solution, even when the notion of "optimum" is well defined. There is no logical reason why

8. W. Edwards (6, 1968).
9. In my comparison of computer and Man, I am leaving out of account the greater sophistication of Man's input and output system, and the parallel processing capabilities of his senses and his limbs. I will be primarily concerned here with thinking, secondarily with perceiving, and not at all with sensing or acting.

72 HERBERT A. SIMON

this needs to be so; it is simply a rather obvious empirical fact about the world we live in – a fact about the relation between the enormous complexity of that world and the modest information-processing capabilities with which Man is endowed. One reason why computers have been so important to Man is that they enlarge a little bit the realm within which his computational powers can match the complexity of the problems. But as the example of the travelling-salesman problem shows, even with the help of the computer, Man soon finds himself outside the area of computable substantive rationality.

The problem space associated with the game of chess is very much smaller than the space associated with the game of life. Yet substantive rationality has so far proved unachievable, both for Man and computer, even in chess. Chess books are full of norms for rational play, but except for catalogues of opening moves, these are procedural rules: how to detect the significant features of a position, what computations to make on these features, how to select plausible moves for dynamic search, and so on.

The psychology of chess playing now has a considerable literature. A pioneer in this research was Professor Adriaan de Groot, of the University of Amsterdam, whose book, *Het Denken van den Schaker,* has stimulated much work on this subject both in Amsterdam, and in our own laboratory at Carnegie-Mellon.[10] These studies have told us a great deal about the thought processes of an expert chess player. First, they have shown how he compensates for his limited computational capacity by searching very selectively through the immense tree of move possibilities, seldom considering as many as 100 branches before making a move. Second, they have shown how he stores in long-term memory a large collection of common patterns of pieces, together with procedures for exploiting the relations that appear in these patterns. The expert chess player's heuristics for selective search and his encyclopedic knowledge of significant patterns are at the core of his procedural rationality in selecting a chess move. Third, the studies have shown how a player forms and modifies his aspirations for a position, so that he can decide when a particular move is "good enough" (satisfices), and can end his search.

Chess is not an isolated example. There is now a large body of data describing human behavior in other problem situations of comparable

10. A. Newell and H.A. Simon (16, 1972); W.G. Chase and H.A. Simon (1, 1973).

complexity. All of the data point in the same direction, and provide essentially the same descriptions of the procedures men use to deal with situations where they are not able to compute an optimum. In all these situations, they use selective heuristics and means-end analysis to explore a small number of promising alternatives. They draw heavily upon past experience to detect the important features of the situation before them, features which are associated in memory with possibly relevant actions. They depend upon aspiration-like mechanisms to terminate search when a satisfactory alternative has been found.

To a moderate extent, this description of choice has been tested outside the laboratory, in even more complex "real-life" situations; and where it has been tested, has held up well. I will only mention as examples Clarkson's wellknown microscopic study of the choices of an investment trust officer,[11] and Peer Soelberg's study of the job search and job choice of graduating management students.[12] I cannot supply you with a large number of more recent examples, possibly because they do not exist, or possibly because my own research has taken me away from the area of field studies in recent years. I would be very pleased if some of you could point out to me examples of such work of which I am unaware; because I know that this is a line of inquiry that has been pursued more vigorously during the past decade in Europe, and particularly in Scandinavia, than in the United States.

Contrast this picture of thought processes with the notion of rationality in the classical theory of the firm in its simplest form. The theory assumes that there is given, in addition to the goal of profit maximization, a demand schedule and a cost curve. The theory then consists of a characterization of the substantively rational production decision: for example that the production quantity is set at the level where marginal cost, calculated from that cost curve, equals marginal revenue, calculated from the demand schedule. The question of whether data are obtainable for estimating these quantities or the demand and cost functions on which they are based, is outside the purview of the theory. If the actual demand and cost curves are given, the actual calculation of the optimum is trivial. This portion of economic theory certainly has nothing to do with procedural rationality.

11. G.P.E. Clarkson (3, 1963).
12. P. Soelberg (19, 1967).

Economics' Concern With Procedural Rationality

In my introductory remarks, I said that while economics has traditionally
concerned itself with substantive rationality, there has been a noticeable
trend, since the Second World War, toward concern also with procedural
rationality. This trend has been brought about by a number of more or
less independent developments.

The Real World of Business and Public Policy

The first of these developments, which predated the War to some extent,
was increasing contact of academic economists with real-world business
environments. An early and important product was the 1939 Hall-Hitch
paper,[13] which advanced the heretical proposition that prices are often
determined by applying a fixed mark-up to average direct cost rather
than by equating them with marginal cost.

I am not concerned here to determine whether Hitch and Hall, or
others who have made similar observations, were right or wrong. My
point is that first-hand contact with business operations leads to
observation of the procedures that are used in reaching decisions, and
not simply the final outcomes. Independently of whether the decision
processes have any importance for the questions to which classical
economics has addressed itself, the phenomena of problem solving and
decision making cannot help but excite the interest of anyone with
intellectual curiosity who encounters them. They represent a fascinating
and important domain of human behavior, which any scientist will wish
to describe and explain.

In the United States, in the decade immediately after the Second
World War, a number of large corporations invited small groups of
academic economists to spend periods of a month or more as "interns"
and observers in their corporate offices. Many young economists had
their first opportunity, in this way, to try their hands at applying the tools
of economic theory to the decisions of a factory department, or a regional
sales office.

They found that businessmen did not need to be advised to "set
marginal cost equal to marginal revenue." Substantive norms of profit

13. R.L. Hall and C.J. Hitch (10, 1939).

maximization helped real decisions only to the extent that appropriate problem-solving procedures could be devised to implement them. What businessmen needed – from anyone who could supply it – was help in inventing and constructing such procedures, including the means for generating the necessary data. How could the marginal productivity of R & D expenditures be measured? Or of advertising expenditures? And if they could not be, what would be reasonable procedures for fixing these quantities? These – and not abstract questions of profit maximization in a simplified model of the firm – were the questions businessmen wrestled with in their decisions.

Matters were no different with the economists who were increasingly called upon by governments to advise on national fiscal and monetary policy, or on economic development plans. We have the notable example here in the Netherlands of Tinbergen's schemes for target planning[14] – a pioneering example of "satisficing," if I may speak anachronistically. In the face of difficult problems of formulating models, designing appropriate and implementable instruments of measurement, taking account of multidimensional criteria and side conditions, questions of optimization generally faded into the background. The rationality of planning and development models was predominately a procedural rationality.

Operations Research

With the end of the War also, businessmen and government departments began to exhibit an interest in the tools of operations research that had been developed for military application during the War. At the same time, operations analysts began to cast about for peacetime problems to which their skills might be applicable. Since the rapid burgeoning of operations research and management science in industry, and the even more rapid development of powerful analytic tools during the first decade after the War is familiar to all of you, it does not need recounting.

The coincidence of the introduction of the digital computer at the same time undoubtedly accelerated these developments. In fact, it is quite unclear whether operations research would have made any considerable impact on practical affairs if the desk calculator had been its only tool.

14. J. Tinbergen (21, 1952).

Operations research and management science did not alter the economic theory of substantive rationality in any fundamental way. With linear programming and activity analysis it did provide a way of handling the old problems and their solutions without the differential calculus, and the classical theorems of marginalism were soon restated in terms of the new formalism.[15]

What was genuinely new for economics in operations research was the concern for procedural rationality – finding efficient procedures for computing actual solutions to concrete decision problems. Let me expand on the specific example with which I am most intimately familiar: decision rules for inventory and work-force smoothing.[16] Here the problem was to devise a decision rule for determining periodically the production level at which a factory should operate. Since the decision for one period was linked to the decisions for the following periods by the inventories carried over, the problem fell in the domain of dynamic programming.

The nub of the problem was to devise a dynamic programming scheme that could actually be carried out using only data that could be obtained in the actual situation. Dynamic programming, in its general formulations, is notoriously extravagant of computational resources. A general algorithm for solving dynamic programming problems would be a non-solution to the real-world decision problem.

The scheme we offered was an algorithm, requiring only a small amount of computing effort, for solving a very special class of dynamic programming problems. The algorithm required the costs to be represented by a quadratic function. This did not mean that we thought real-world cost functions were quadratic; it meant that we thought that many cost functions could be reasonably approximated by a quadratic, and that the deviations from the actual function would not lead to seriously non-optimal decisions. This assumption must, of course, be justified in each individual case, before an application can safely be made. Not only did the quadratic function provide good computational efficiency, but it also greatly reduced the data requirements, because it could be proved that, with this function, only the expected values of predicted variables, and not their higher moments, affected the optimal decision.[17]

15. R. Dorfman, P.A. Samuelson and R.M. Solow (5, 1958).
16. C.C. Holt, F. Modigliani, J.F. Muth and H.A. Simon (11, 1960).
17. It is interesting that this same dynamic programming procedure for quadratic cost

This is only part of what was involved in devising a procedurally rational method for making these inventory and production decisions. The problems had also to be solved of translating an aggregate "production level" into specific production schedules for individual products. I will not, however, go into these other aspects of the matter.

Observe of our solution that we constructed a quite classical model for profit maximization, but we did not have the illusion that the model reflected accurately all the details of the real-world situation. All that was expected of the solution was that the *optimal* decision in the world of the model be a *good* decision in the real world. There was no claim that the solution was substantively optimal, but rather that formal optimization in the dynamic programming model was an effective procedural technique for making acceptable decisions (*i.e.,* decisions better than those that would be made without this formal apparatus).

Some operations research methods take the other horn of this dilemma: they retain more of the real-world detail in the model, but then give up, for reasons of computational feasibility, the goal of searching for an optimum, and seek a satisfactory solution instead.[18]

Thus, the demands of computability led to two kinds of deviation from classical optimization: simplification of the model to make computation of an "optimum" feasible, or, alternatively, searching for satisfactory, rather than optimal choices. I am inclined to regard both of these solutions as instances of satisficing behavior rather than optimization. To be sure, we can *formally* view these as optimizing procedures by introducing, for example, a cost of computation and a marginal return from computation, and using these quantities to compute the optimal stopping-point for the computation. But the important difference between the new procedures and the classical ones remain. The problem has been shifted from one of characterizing the substantively optimal solution to one of devising practicable computation procedures for making reasonable choices.

functions was invented independently and simultaneously by H. Theil of the Rotterdam School of Economics. See H. Theil (20, 1958). The Rotterdam group was also concerned with concrete applications – in this case to national economic planning in the Netherlands and hence gave a high priority to the demands of procedural rationality in the solutions it developed.

18. I have already mentioned the pioneering work of J. Tinbergen in the Netherlands, who employed national planning models that aimed at target values of key variables instead of an optimum.

Imperfect Competition

More than a century ago, Cournot identified a problem that has become
the permanent and ineradicable scandal of economic theory. He
observed that where a market is supplied by only a few producers, the
notion of profit maximization is ill-defined. The choice that would be
substantively rational for each actor depends on the choices made by the
other actors; none can choose without making assumptions about how
others will choose.

Cournot proposed a particular solution for the problem, which
amounted to an assumption about the *procedure* each actor would
follow: each would observe the quantities being produced by his
competitors, and would assume these quantities to be fixed in his own
calculations. The Cournot solution has often been challenged, and many
alternative solutions have been proposed – conjectural variations, the
kinky demand curve, market leadership, and others. All of them rest on
postulates about the decision process, in particular, about the
information each decision maker will take into account, and the
assumptions he will make about the reactions of the others to his
behavior.

I have referred to the theory of imperfect competition as a "scandal"
because it has been treated as such in economics, and because it is
generally conceded that no defensible formulation of the theory stays
within the framework of profit maximization and substantive rationality.
Game theory, initially hailed as a possible way out, provided only a
rigorous demonstration of how fundamental the difficulties really are.

If perfect competition were the rule in the markets of our modern
economy, and imperfect competition and oligopoly rare exceptions, the
scandal might be ignored. Every family, after all, has some distant
relative it would prefer to forget. But imperfect competition is not a
"distant relative," it is the characteristic form of market structure in a
large part of the industries in our economy.

In the literature on oligopoly and imperfect competition one can trace a
gradual movement toward more and more explicit concern with the
processes used to reach decisions, even to the point – unusual in most
other areas of economics – of trying to obtain empirical data about these
processes. There remains, however, a lingering reluctance to acknowledge the impossiblility of discovering at last "The Rule" of substantively rational behavior for the oligopolist. Only when the hope of that

discovery has been finally extinguished will it be admitted that understanding imperfect competition means understanding procedural rationality.

This change in viewpoint will have large effects on many areas of economic research. There has been a great burgeoning, for example, of "neo-classical" theories of investment – theories that undertake to deduce the rates of investment of business firms from the assumptions of profit maximization and substantive rationality. Central to such theories is the concept of "desired capital" – that is, the volume of capital that would maximize profits. Jorgenson, for example, typically derives "desired capital" by an argument that assumes a fixed price for the firm's products and a production function of the Cobb-Douglas type, all in the absence of uncertainty.[19] Under these assumptions, he shows that the optimal level of capital is proportional to output.

Since the data which Jorgenson and others use to test these theories of investment derive mostly from oligopolistic industries, their definitions of rationality are infected with precisely the difficulties we have been discussing. Can we speak of the capital desired by General Motors or the American Can Company without considering their expectations for size and share of market or the interactions of these expectations with price policies and with the responses of competitors?[20] Under conditions of imperfect competition, one can perhaps speak of the procedural rationality of an investment strategy, but surely not of its substantive rationality. At most, the statistical studies of investment behavior show that some business firms relate their investments to output; they do not show that such behavior is predictable from an objective theory of profit maximization. (And if that is what is being demonstrated, what is the advantage of doing it by means of elaborate statistical studies of public data, rather than by making inquiries or observations of the actual decision processes in the firms themselves?)

Expectations and Uncertainty

Making guesses about the behavior of a competitor in an oligopolistic industry is simply a special case of forming expectations in order to make

19. D.W. Jorgenson (13, 1963).
20. R.M. Cyert, E.A. Feigenbaum and J.G. March (4, 1959).

decisions under uncertainty. As economics has moved from statics to dynamics – to business cycle theory, growth theory, dynamic investment theory, theory of innovation and technological change – it has become more and more explicit in its treatment of uncertainty.

Uncertainty, however, exists not in the outside world, but in the eye and mind of the beholder. We need not enter into philosophical arguments as to whether quantum-mechanical uncertainty lies at the very core of nature, for we are not concerned with events at the level of the atom. We are concerned with how men behave rationally in a world where they are often unable to predict the relevant future with accuracy. In such a world, their ignorance of the future prevents them from behaving in a substantively rational manner; they can only adopt a rational choice procedure, including a rational procedure for forecasting or otherwise adapting to the future.

In a well-known paper, my former colleague, John F. Muth,[21] proposed to objectify the treatment of uncertainty in economics by removing it from the decision maker to nature. His hypothesis is "that expectations of firms (or, more generally, the subjective probability distribution of outcomes) tend to be distributed, for the same information set, about the prediction of the theory (or the 'objective' probability distributions of outcomes)." In application this hypothesis involves setting the expected value (in the statistical sense) of a future economic variable equal to its predicted value.

Muth's proposal is ingenious and important. Let us see exactly what it means. Suppose that a producer has an accurate knowledge of the consumer demand function and the aggregate supply function of producers in his industry. Then he can estimate the equilibrium price – the price at which the quantities that producers will be induced to offer will just balance demand. Muth proposes essentially that each producer takes this equilibrium price as his price forecast. If random shocks with zero expected value are now introduced into the supply equation, and if producers continue to act on price forecasts made in the manner just described, then the forecast price will equal the expected value of the actual price.

Notice that the substantively rational behavior for the producer would be to produce the quantity that would be optimal for the price that is *actually* realized. The assumption of Muth's model that the random

21. J.F. Muth (15, 1961).

shocks are completely unpredictable makes this impossible. The producer then settles for a procedure that under the assumptions of the model will give him an unbiased prediction of the price. Nor, as Muth himself notes, will this procedure be optimal, even under uncertainty, unless the loss function is quadratic.

Uncertainty plays the same innocuous role in the optimal linear production smoothing rule I described earlier,[22] which is closely related to Muth's analysis. Here the explicit assumption of a quadratic cost function makes it possible to prove that only the expected values and not the higher moments of predicted variables are relevant to decision. This does not mean that action based on unbiased estimates is substantively rational, independently of the variances of those estimates. On the contrary, performance can always be improved if estimation errors can be reduced.

Even if it turns out to be empirically true that the forecasts of business firms and other economic actors are unbiased forecasts of future events, this finding will have modest implications for the nature of human rationality. Unbiased estimation can be a component of all sorts of rational and irrational behavior rules.

In an earlier section I commented on the psychological evidence as to human choice in the face of uncertainty. Only in the very simplest situations does behavior conform reasonably closely to the predictions of classical models of rationality. But even this evidence exaggerates the significance of those classical models for human affairs; for all of the experiments are limited to situations where the alternatives of choice are fixed in advance, and where information is available only from precisely specified sources.

Once we become interested in the procedures – the rational processes – that economic actors use to cope with uncertainty, we must broaden our horizons further. Uncertainty not only calls forth forecasting procedures; it also calls forth a whole range of actions to reduce uncertainty, or at least to make outcomes less dependent upon it. These actions are of at least four kinds:
1. Intelligence actions to improve the data on which forecasts are based, to obtain new data, and to improve the forecasting models;
2. Actions to buffer the effects of forecast errors: holding inventories, insuring, and hedging, for example;

22. C.C. Holt, F. Modigliani, J.F. Muth and H.A. Simon (11, 1960).

3. Actions to reduce the sensitivity of outcomes to the behavior of competitors: steps to increase product and market differentiation, for example;
4. Actions to enlarge the range of alternatives whenever the perceived alternatives involve high risk.

A theory of rational choice in the face of uncertainty will have to encompass not only the topic of forecasting, but these other topics as well. Moreover, it will have to say something about the circumstances under which people will (or should) pursue one or the other of these lines of action.

Confronting a list of contingencies of this sort fills many economists with malaise. How can an unique answer be found to the problem of choice if all of these considerations enter it? How much more attractive is classical economics, in allowing strong conclusions to be drawn from a few *a priori* assumptions, with little need for empirical observation!

Alas, we must take the world as it is. As economics becomes more concerned with procedural rationality, it will necessarily have to borrow from psychology or build for itself a far more complete theory of human cognitive processes than it has had in the past. Even if our interest lies in normative rather than descriptive economics, we will need such a theory. There are still many areas of decision – particularly those that are ill-structured – where human cognitive processes are more effective than the best available optimization techniques or artificial intelligence methods. Every Class A chessplayer plays a far better game than any existing chess-playing computer program. A great deal can still be learned about effective decision procedures by studying how humans make choices.

The human mind is programmable: it can acquire an enormous variety of different skills, behavior patterns, problem-solving repertoires, and perceptual habits. Which of these it will acquire in any particular case is a function of what it has been taught and what it has experienced. We can expect substantive rationality only in situations that are sufficiently simple as to be transparent to this mind. In all other situations, we must expect that the mind will use such imperfect information as it has, will simplify and represent the situation as it can, and will make such calculations as are within its powers. We cannot expect to predict what it will do in such situations unless we know what information it has, what forms of representation it prefers, and what algorithms are available to it.

There seems to be no escape. If economics is to deal with uncertainty, it will have to understand how human beings in fact behave in the face of uncertainty, and by what limits of information and computability they are bound.

The Empirical Study of Decision Making

As I remarked earlier, since my own recent research has removed me from the study of decision making in organization settings, I am not in a position to comment on the current state of our empirical knowledge of organizational decision making.

In trying to understand procedural rationality as it relates to economics, we do not have to limit ourselves, however, to organizational studies. I have already commented upon the understanding we have gained, during the past twenty years, of human problem solving processes – mostly by study in the laboratory, using puzzle-like tasks. Most of these studies have used naive subjects performing tasks with which they had little or no previous experience. In one case, however – the research on chessplaying – an intensive investigation has been made of highly skilled, professional performance, and a body of theory constructed to explain that performance.

Chess may seem a rather esoteric domain, but perhaps business is no less esoteric to those who do not practice it. There is no reason to believe that the basic human faculties that a chess professional of twenty years' experience brings to bear upon his decisions are fundamentally different from the faculties used by an experienced professional businessman. In fact, to the extent that comparable studies of business decision making have been carried out, they give us reason to believe in the basic similarity of those faculties.

On the basis of the research on chessplayers, what appears to distinguish expert from novice is not only that the former has a great quantity and variety of information, but that his perceptual experience enables him to detect familiar patterns in the situations that confront him, and by recognizing these patterns, to retrieve speedily a considerable amount of relevant information from long-term memory.[23] It is this perceptual experience that permits the chessmaster to play, and usually win, many simultaneous games against weaker opponents, taking only a

23. A.D. de Groot (8, 1965); W.G. Chase and H.A. Simon (2, 1973).

few seconds for each move. It is very likely similar perceptual experience about the world of business that enables the executive to react "intuitively," without much awareness of his own cognitive processes, to business situations as they arise.

There is no reason to suppose that the theory of cognitive processes that will emerge from the empirical study of the chessmaster's or businessman's decision processes will be "neat" or "elegant," in the sense that the Laws of Motion or the axioms of classical utility theory are neat and elegant. If we are to draw an analogy with the natural sciences, we might expect the theory of procedural rationality to resemble molecular biology, with its rich taxonomy of mechanisms, more closely than either classical mechanics or classical economics. But as I suggested earlier, an empirical science cannot remake the world to its fancy: it can only describe and explain the world as it is.

A major source of complication in theories of professional decision making is the dependence of decisions upon large quantities of stored information and previously learned decision procedures. This is true not only at an individual psychological level, but also at a social and historical level. The play of two chessplayers differs as a result of differences in what they know about chess: no less do the decisions of two businessmen differ as a result of differences in what they know about business. Moreover Bobby Fisher, in 1972, played chess differently from Paul Morphy, in 1861. Much of that latter difference was the result of the knowledge of the game that has cumulated over the century through the collective experience of the whole society of professional chessplayers.

Economics, like chess, is inevitably culture-bound and history-bound. A business firm equipped with the tools of operations research does not make the same decisions as it did before it possessed those tools. The considerable secular decline over recent years of inventories held by American firms is probably due in considerable part to this enhancement of rationality by new theory and new computational tools.

Economics is one of the sciences of the artificial.[24] It is a description and explanation of human institutions, whose theory is no more likely to remain invariant over time than the theory of bridge design. Decision processes, like all other aspects of economic institutions, exist inside human heads. They are subject to change with every change in what human beings know, and with every change in their means of calculation.

24. H.A. Simon (18, 1969).

For this reason the attempt to predict and prescribe human economic behavior by deductive inference from a small set of unchallengeable premises must fail and has failed.

Economics will progress as we deepen our understanding of human thought processes; and economics will change as human individuals and human societies use progressively sharpened tools of thought in making their decisions and designing their institutions. A body of theory for procedural rationality is consistent with a world in which human beings continue to think and continue to invent; a theory of substantive rationality is not.

Conclusion

In this paper I have contrasted the concept of substantive rationality that has dominated classical economics with the concept of procedural rationality that has prevailed in psychology. I have described also some of the concerns of economics that have forced that discipline to begin to concern itself with procedural rationality – with the actual processes of cognition, and with the limits on the human organism that give those processes their peculiar character.

The shift from theories of substantive rationality to theories of procedural rationality requires a basic shift in style, from an emphasis on deductive reasoning from a tight system of axioms to an emphasis on detailed empirical exploration of complex algorithms of thought. Undoubtedly the uncongeniality of the latter style to economists has slowed the transition. As economics becomes more and more involved in the study of uncertainty, more and more concerned with the complex actuality of business decision making, the transition will become inevitable. Wider and wider areas of economics will replace the oversimplified assumptions of the omniscient decision maker with a realistic characterization of the limits on Man's rationality, and the consequences of those limits for his economic behavior.

References

1. Chase, W.G. and H.A. Simon, "Skill in Chess," *American Scientist*, LXI (1973), pp. 394-403.
2. Chase, W.G. and H.A. Simon, "Perception in Chess," *Cognitive Psychology*, IV (1973), pp. 55-81.

3. Clarkson, G.P.E., "A Model of the Trust Investment Process," in Feigenbaum and Feldman (eds.) *Computers and Thought*, New York, 1963.
4. Cyert, R.M., E.A. Feigenbaum and J.G. March, "Models in a Behavioral Theory of the Firm," *Behavioral Science*, IV (1959), pp. 81-95.
5. Dorfman, R., P.A. Samuelson and R.M. Solow, *Linear Programming and Economic Analysis*, New York, 1958.
6. Edwards, W., "Conservatism in Human Information Processing," in B. Kleinmuntz (ed.), *Formal Representation of Human Judgment*, New York, 1968, pp. 17-52.
7. Feldman, J., "Simulation of Behavior in the Binary Choice Experiment," in Feigenbaum and Feldman (eds.), *Computer and Thought*, New York, 1963.
8. Groot, A.D. de, *Thought and Choice in Chess*, Den Haag, 1965.
9. Gould, J. and W.L. Kolb (eds.), *A Dictionary of the Social Sciences*, Glencoe, 1964.
10. Hall, R.L. and C.J. Hitch, "Price Theory and Business Behavior," *Oxford Economic Papers*, II (1939), pp. 12-45.
11. Holt, C.C., F. Modigliani, J.F. Muth and H.A. Simon, *Planning Production, Inventories and Work Force*, Englewood Cliffs, N.J., 1960.
12. James, W., *Principles of Psychology*, 1890.
13. Jorgenson, D.W., "Capital Theory and Investment Behavior," *American Economic Review, Papers and Proceedings*, LIII (1963), pp. 247-259.
14. Kahneman, D. and A. Tversky, "On the Psychology of Prediction," *Psychological Review*, LXXX (1973), pp. 237-251.
15. Muth, J.F., "Rational Expectations and the Theory of Price Movements," *Econometrica*, XXIX (1961), pp. 315-335.
16. Newell, A. and H.A. Simon, *Human Problem Solving*, Englewood Cliffs, N.J., 1972.
17. Rapaport, A. and T.S. Wallsten, "Individual Decision Behavior," *Annual Review of Psychology*, XXIII (1972), pp. 131-176.
18. Simon, H.A., *The Sciences of the Artificial*, Cambridge, Mass., 1969.
19. Soelberg, P., *A Study of Decision Making: Job Choice*, Ph.D. Dissertation, Carnegie-Mellon University, 1967.
20. Theil, H., *Economic Forecasts and Policy*, Amsterdam, 1958.
21. Tinbergen, J., *On the Theory of Economic Policy*, Amsterdam, 1952.

Management science and human values: a retrospect

C. West Churchman

Although I am to discuss the role of management science in the past 25 years, I thought it would be most interesting to this faculty that is celebrating its 25 anniversary to discuss the role of economics in management science. Hence, I would like to talk about some aspects of what I think to be the contribution of economic theory to the development of management science in the past 25 years, as well as its prospects for the future. Herbert Simon has told us that economists have to become interested in procedural reasoning. I am going to tell you that economists have to become a lot more interested in what I call teleological reasoning.

By teleological reasoning I mean something that in history and philosophy has always been important, not so much to decide how we are to attain the goals that we are interested in, as individuals or as society, but whether these goals are appropriate ones. Rationality is attached to that question just as much in the history of philosophy as it is attached to the means of attaining goals. Is it reasonable to talk about the proper goals that we humans are to pursue, and if so, then what does reason tell us about these goals?

Before getting into that, I need a backtrack, these 25 years, to discuss the beginnings of management science, and what was happening at that period of time. Of course, both economics and management science are much older than 25 years. I trace the origins of management science back to the *I Ching*, which was written about 2000 or 1000 B.C. I regard it to be one of the earliest texts in management science; it even used a little computer; one threw the yarrow sticks in certain ways and needed somebody's expert experience in "programming" the sticks in order to interpret them properly, and thus direct one to the correct model for the manager to use in order to obtain helpful advice.

But something happened in the post World War II period, which I think legitimately characterized a distinct episode in the long history of management science, and I shall begin at that period. Around 1950 there was undoubtedly an upsurge of interest in the question whether or not the scientist can help the manager in the difficult problems that he faces. Even in the industrial area it was not the first time the question has been asked, but it was asked in a certain way in the early fifties that has generated the history of the 25 years since.

There are lots of origins to that upsurge of interest in management science at that time. When I explained to some of my economics colleagues that I was going to Groningen to discuss the contributions of economics to management science, I asked them what they thought the contribution of economics was, and they said almost to a man, very modestly, "well we began it all, and we were really responsible for carrying it all out." Actually, that "modest" claim on their part does not hold much historical justification. The real origins of the upsurge of interest in the use of science for the study of management problems, I think, goes back to Operations Research in World War II. That development began in Great Britain where certain people in academic institutions said to themselves, "we are trained scientists and some of the problems that the R.A.F. and others are facing clearly have a kind of scientific flavour to them. Possibly we, with our scientific background, can assist them." So these people left the ivory tower and went out to help in various kinds of problems that the British were facing during the Battle of Britain. In particular, the very first studies were on "early warning radar," in which in effect the scientists said that the whole method of detecting that the Luftwaffe was coming, and relating this information to the way in which the anti-aircraft batteries were set up, was irrational. In fact the anti-aircraft batteries were starting to work at their heaviest when the R.A.F. was getting up there to fight the Luftwaffe. The consequence was that the R.A.F. was getting knocked down as frequently as the German planes. It took some common sense to see that maybe you should not start the anti-aircraft at the time that you had thought was the most appropriate. Instead you wait tensely for a while, until your aircraft are aloft. A lot of this was good common sense, but a lot did consist of some good measurements procedures. After World War II and the success of Operations Research in both U.K. and U.S.A., there was a lot of speculation about what the implications of the war experience might be for other types of management. Now if you read the history of Operations Research during World War II, you will see that the role of the economists during that period was very minimal. It was not mainly economists that did this kind of scientific war research. The principal actors were primarily physical and biological scientists, and a variety of others.

Often the criterion of whether or not to tackle a problem was that unless you thought you could improve the system threefold on some reasonable scale, then you should not bother to do the Operations Research study. I contrast such a criterion with a speech that I heard George Dantzig give in the early 1950's, when he was telling us about the success of linear programming in the oil industry. He said that the use of linear programming in the oil industry had probably increased their efficiency about 1%, that is quite a contrast from the threefold increase in value used in World War II. George went on hastily to point out that the oil industry is making billions of dollars and 1% of billions of dollars is still a lot of dollars. The point is that World War II Operations Research was not based on economic criteria, and yet I think it could be claimed that it was the spark that gave rise to the increased interest in the use of models and scientific studies for the help of management.

Of course there were other contributors to the development of Operations Research and management science; they even go back to the early part of this century. Erlang in his early work on the telephone company developed the basis of waiting line theory as we understand it today. Wilson and others developed the basis of inventory theory in the 1910's and the 1920's. I also include in the contributions to the early developments of the management science in the 1950's the input-output analysis that was conducted before World War II by Leontief and others. And finally I should mention philosophical ideas about the need to develop "whole system" thinking as we study social systems.

I should now like to talk about two contributions that economic theory made, once we began to move into the management science of the 1950's. Before I do that, I might mention a little bit about the labels that were used in the late 1940's and the early 1950's. Operations Research was the label that came out of World War II experiences. It was not a mysterious label at all to the military. Both in the U.K. and the U.S.A. the military is divided up into various kinds of functions, one of which is "operations." The Operations Research teams mainly conducted research on military operations, and so it was not surprising that they were called "Operations Research" teams.

As we began to think in the early 1950's about applying Operations Research in industry, the label itself began to make less sense because industrial organizations do not have divisions that are called "operations divisions" of the company. We normally think of production and marketing and finance and so on, so the label Operations Research turned out to be a kind of a mystery label. It actually worked very well for us; there is nothing that managers get more fascinated by than by labels they do not understand. The first conference on Operations Research in industry was held at Case Institute of Technology in 1951. We invited industrial managers to come and some 200 suckers appeared on the scene. They were suckers, because we had absolutely nothing to sell; there was no "Operations Research in industry." This was nothing but a conference of promises, so to speak.

But when the success of that conference became apparent, then even at the conference, a number of people said what we really ought to do now is start an organization, an Operations Research Society. The decision was made that one thing such a society should do is safeguard the "Profession" of Operations Research, which was a big laugh because there was no profession but just a few scientific characters going out helping managers trying to solve their problems. But there is nothing like success to make you think you are important, and so it was decided that one of the main functions of the society would be to make sure that people did not claim they were operations researchers when they really were not operations researchers. Hence, it was voted to institute classes of membership; there was the high class of operations researchers who were called fellows; they were fellows because they had "done OR" during World War II. Then there were members and a very low class people called associate members. The founders did not know what criterion to use, excepting that most fellows had to agree that a candidate fellow had done a good job.

A number of us said how ridiculous this all was, that this is no way to start a society which should have an open membership.

Because we were defeated in that effort, we had a second thought, namely, that we should start a more general society which would have no criterion of membership. Whether the label "management science" was well selected or not was one of the fiercest arguments I have ever heard in a "founding father's" meeting. In any event, we called it "The Institute of Management Science." The label was probably not the best description and many of us today would say we would have been much happier if it had been called system science, or something less specific to management per se. I should add that The Institute of Management

Science also came about because some economists were not able to publish their papers in respectable economic journals.

That is enough of historical background on labels except to say that in 25 years the distinction between Operations Research and management science has never been clear and indeed the two labels now mean much the same thing both in universities and industry.

There are many ways in which science can be turned to help managers make better decisions. I am interested tonight, as a historical matter, in pulling back a little and looking at the contributions of various disciplines but specifically economics in the development of management science in the last 25 years. One of them I should like to highlight because of my interest as a philosopher. No doubt the economists have played a big role in regional, national and international planning, by trying to develop economic theory that would be helpful to the managers of the world. I think these developments are fascinating to look at and to appraise, but I am less interested in them than I am in one major contribution that was made in the foundation of management science by the economists. It was to supply the early management scientists in the 1950's with a value base which we desperately needed: a way of valuating different alternative plans or actions. If you examine the disciplines of the early 1950's to find which ones had something to offer the management scientists in the way of a value scale that could be used in applied research, it really was only economics that had a useful theory of evaluation. Certainly not sociology. Sociology talked a great deal at that time about human values, but there was no way of relating sociological literature to the job of going in and looking at the manager's inventory problem, or pricing problem, or, in the public sector, problems of where to put streets and hospitals, and so on. Nothing that was happening in sociological literature of the 1940's was in the least bit amenable to help guide us in evaluation.

Now, to the economists in the audience, I ought to explain immediately that I am not an economist. I am a researcher at Berkeley and the bureaucracy has to give researchers some kind of a label. For a while I was labeled as a research economist, because I was in the business school, and I complained. I said I am not an economist, and they said what are you anyway? I said I am a philosopher, and they said all right, then you are a "research philosopher." So I apologize to the economists in the audience for any ignorance I may display about economic theory. I am only going to discuss what I think management science has meant by utility theory. Its real father was David Hume, in the 18th century. Hume was not the first to suggest that human values can be considered in terms of utility, but he probably gave the clearest expression of the idea.

He came upon his ideas at a time when people were beginning to recognize that good common decent Englishman behaviour was not regarded as all that good, common or decent in other countries. The anthropological studies that were being made in the latter part of the 18th century showed radically divergent standards of behaviour. Hume took these results rather seriously, specially since he was a Scotchman (and anything he could do to embarrass an Englishman was all to the good), by pointing out that other cultures have different values, and that what seems to be decent and proper to an Englishman, may not be decent and proper in other cultures. It would have been rather indecent of you tonight to arrive completely naked and listen to this talk. On the other hand there are plenty of cultures where something approximating that behaviour would have been a respectable way of behaving here.

Hume had got the idea that when we were talking about human values we were really talking about the basic utility of the people. And if it is useful to dress, then you dress, and when it is not useful to dress, you do not dress. If it is useful to bring up sickly babies, then you do it; if it is not useful to you, you do not. Out of that idea came the basic notions of utility. Hume himself, I think, was probably more astute than most latter utilitarians in recognizing that the basic idea was *utility*. Bentham, who came a little later, argued in effect that utility was to be translated into "pleasure." But if you are a masochist you may attain maximum utility by punching various holes in yourself. It is a "useful" value to you if there is a satisfactory amount of pain.

Hume was really after what I would call an "enabling philosophy of values." The human race has a multiplicity of values, and collectively we are not about to settle on which objectives are rational and which are irrational. But one thing we can agree upon, among us all, is that which *enables* us to gain whatever it is we as individuals wish to gain. This is the common value we all share. And there is no need to introduce pleasure, happiness, unhappiness, or whatever. The main point that he was making is that we have one common value we all share together which is the capability of doing whatever it is each individual wants to do.

In case our objectives conflict, then there is a basic problem, but that is not the end of the matter.

Stated in economic terms, the argument is that every individual carries with him a measure which describes the way in which he would allocate his preferences for commodities. But that is the economist way of describing, because many economists were interested in the economics of commodities. We as management scientists immediately generalized on that and said that any organization carries with it a basic utility function which translates the physical condition that that organization finds itself in, into one utility measure. And, of course, dollars or guilders would be an obvious reference we had in mind, because the more dollars or guilders you have the better off you are and the more things you can do. So it made perfectly good sense for us then to use the money system. But the background of money is the basic human utilitarian system.

Utility theory encompasses the concept of opportunity costing, which is central to all practising management science. We do not often know how to measure opportunity cost, but we do realize that we are always dealing, not with accounting costs, but with opportunity costs.

Thus we borrowed from economic theory the notions of opportunity costs and opportunity demands and saw that our whole enterprise of working with the business firms or in the government area dealt with these basic notions that stem from utility theory. This enabled us to set up mathematical models and to identify the measurement problems we were faced with. For example, in a typical inventory problem one can identify the cost measurement problems: what is the cost of ordering, what is the cost of shortage, what is the cost of holding inventory and so on, all of those costs had to be represented in utility terms, *i.e.,* in terms of lost opportunities. I would also say we took from micro-economics the theory of the allocation of resources, which in principle tells how to allocate resources for specific goals. Many of the earlier models that were used in Operation Research were simply applications of the economic theory of resource allocation.

Tonight I want to try an "appreciation" of utility theory. The word "appreciation" in English is an extremely rich one in meaning. It does not mean just praising something; it means that one struggles to define both the positive values as well as the negative values.

I want to begin with a very positive appreciation of what utility theory does, what I think its real strengths are, and why it was not just a kind of attractive alternative, but a very plausible and strong one available to us. Just to repeat, its principle is that every individual carries around with him a way of evaluating between alternative states of the world. And if certain actions were adopted and we can predict what the state of the world will be as a result of those, we can begin to measure his utility for that state of the world. This is not necessarily as far as many economists have been willing to go, but certainly it is what the management scientist had to do, whether he liked it or not. So if the manager went into this new product, we had to say, well if you do, you get this state of the world and we will try to estimate what the value of that state of the world is for you. We were aware of the various things that Jeremy Bentham pointed out back in the 18th century, about the need for considering uncertainty and for discounting for future value against present value straight out of the economic theory of utilities. It was a very powerful way of doing things, we also generalized the theory to apply not only to individuals, but to organizations, cities, regions, states, nations, and so on. Every city implicitly has some utility function that translates what is going on in that city into a measure of value of that city. We firmly believe that that was so. In the culture of Operation Research and management science, most practising Operation Research types believe in this principle.

I have to tell you a story in this regard. In one period in the history of the city of New York, one operation researcher, George Feeney, convinced Mayor Lindsay, the Mayor of the city of New York, and his staff, that they could greatly benefit by having Operations Research people come and look at the problems of the city of New York. They were very interested in doing it, and out of that came an Operation Research Council for the city of New York, where we were supposed to advise the city on various kinds of study that should be made. At the first meeting of our council, Mayor Lindsay had graced us with his presence. As we talked, Mayor Lindsay told us about all the problems of the city of New York and he talked much too long about it, but in any event, eventually George Feeney turned to the Mayor and said, "Now Mayor Lindsay, you realize we are operations researchers, and we are committed to the principle of a measure of performance of an organization. We believe there is such a thing as measure performance. Would you kindly tell us, what you would consider to be the measure performance of the city of New York in any one year"? At which point Lindsay looked at George, I guess it must have been 30 seconds, but it felt like 5 minutes, and then went on to talk about something else. He was not about to give the measure of performance of the city of New York; there might have been somebody there that could have used it against him, whatever measure of performance he had suggested.

As management scientists, we were committed to this notion that there is a unifying measure of performance for any organization that we studied. We may not always be able to estimate it, but at least it exists, we eventually expect to find a suitable measure for any organization, and we can make comparisons between alternatives along that unifying scale. Not only did we believe that, but I am also convinced that most of us believed that that measure of performance was not a relative value; it was an ethical value, just as David Hume earlier claimed it to be. It represented what for an organization was the best thing for the organization to attain, in order to enrich the lives of every individual in that organization, or the clients of the organization. So it represented all of the relevant matters, like being able to supply people with food, shelter, comfortable living, transportation, education, health, and all the other dimensions, including being able to walk along the street without being killed. All of those got into that basic measure of performance in some way or other.

We were borrowing therefore not only from economics a way of measuring how well a given alternative works out, but also an ethical base for our considerations. We did not think that we were just improving this organization for its own sake. The measure of performance of the city of New York has relevance to the measure of performance for the state of New York, for the nation and for the internation. We were committed to the notion that utility theory had not only a practical but also a sound ethical base. And we did generalize therefore from the individual to the total community, city, or whatever it may be. That assumption that we were borrowing became the base, as many of you know, for many of the models that we use in Operations Research. Where we are maximizing some measure of performances as a function of various resource variables and various constraint equations, all of the various values can be unified, back into one single measure of performance. It is one reason incidently why from the management science point of view, the suggestion that we add social indicators is ridiculous. Social indicators were suggested by Harvard's Ray Bauer and others, who said that we ought to add on to the so-called economic values some other values that were more of a social character, like how do people get along together, or how do they communicate to one another, and so on. From the point of view of utility theory that is just like deciding to add honey to sugar, I mean if it is already sweet enough, do not add any more. If you think communication is an important property in a social organization, and that more communication should take place between individuals, then we should in principle be able to state its utility value, because all of it gets put together in the unifying measure of performance. There is no such thing as separating the economic considerations from the so called social considerations.

Of course, not all economists recognize this point. I have even heard an economist get up and say that in addition to the economic considerations we must also have some human considerations. If they had listened to themselves, they would have heard themselves saying that economics is nonhuman, and therefore we must add to nonhuman economics some human properties. All values should be incorporated in utility theory. If you make a decision, whatever it is, it includes all of the values. We can even do an imputed estimate of your notion of the utility of say communication or safety, or whatever, in terms of the decisions that you make. We have even done such things as evaluating the cost of life, as after all there is a limit people who are willing to pay for human safety. In the United States of America we believe it is perfectly appropriate to sacrifice 50,000 lives for the sake of getting automobiles along highways for a year. We do not cut the driver's hearts out; we just smash them in various ways so that traffic may proceed. We management scientists saw a difference between what economists might talk about as economic values, but when you come down to the real application of utility theory it is a unified theory of values. And since it is, it means unification of future values against past values, against current values. Now, all the foregoing is an appreciation of utility theory; it was a very positive contribution to where we were in the early 50's.

Now suppose we examine the critical problems. It is interesting to note that what bothers us in management science, and began to bother us more and more about utility theory, does not seem to have been what bothers many economists, as I understand their literature. Since I am not standing as an expert in economics, I will only mention a few of the things that at least I have heard bother economists. One is the intercomparison of utilities. Each one of us carries around his utility function and then of course we try to aggregate utilities in certain ways; by comparing individual utilities, adding them, etc. That method never did bother the management scientist. There are various reasons why it did not. I think the fact that it bothered the economists is a little bit silly. They somehow got trapped in the old-fashioned empirist notion, which was that I and I alone know my own toothache, and you can not know my toothache the way I know my toothache, which is a lot of damned nonsense. I can know your toothache in lots of ways you do not know your toothache. And if your spouse has ever had a toothache, you may very well know his/her toothache better than he/she does.

The problem of utility comparisons seems never to have bothered the management scientists, and surely does not bother me, but it seems to have bothered the economist a good deal. It did not ever really get into our literature, no more than did the philosopher's worry that bothered them in the 19th century. They could understand maximizing your own utility, but what motivates you to maximize society its utilities? That became the big subject matter of English ethical philosophy of the 19th century, of people like Henri Sidgwick: what carries me from my own individual selfish utility maximization out to society? That never bothered the management scientist. We wanted to aggregate utilities over social organizations, and to say that we ought to optimize over the total organization. This also I think, in some ways, is really not an interesting philosophical argument, though it always helps when you try to interest your philosophy students in learning about ethics. They are often eager to talk about egoism versus altruism. In management science there was no doubt that we were on the altruistic side, and that issue never became a cumbersome one for us.

Last, just to go quickly through this, Arrow's "impossibility theorem" that came out in the early 1950s, was in effect the start of a whole incredible stream of articles in economic journals, but never bothered the practising management scientist. I cannot think of any Operations Research study that worried about whether or not it was reasonable to expect a democratic utility function to operate.

But there were, for us, some serious difficulties in utility theory. The first one, I think, is a very serious one, but I do not think the blame is to be laid at economist's feet at all. It is a kind of perverted utilization of economic theory in cost-benefit analysis. The point is that somebody along the line has been advertising that social programs can be evaluated by assessing the economic benefits or, to make it more general, social benefits, and the social costs, and, on that basis provide the decision makers, especially governmental decision makers, the "true" value of important social programs. Cost-benefit analysis is done now by a number of consulting firms in the States. I think the deficiencies in these analyses constitute a very serious matter in the United States at the present time. The Office of Management and Budget officers are going around asking various agencies about their programs, in education, health, transportation, and so on, and in effect they are asking for a cost-benefit number. Now to do an analysis of this kind, to really get out the true benefits of a program, you have to know a great deal. You have to know a great deal about the nature of the program, what it is doing to people. But, let us face it, we really do not know, for example, what education is all about. We do not know what it does to people. We certainly do not know, just by my standing up in front of a group of 25 students, week after week, what the effect of that is on their future lives, or on any kind of economic benefits they may have. We do not know much about education at this stage in human history, and we are fairly young at it anyhow. We have not really had the years that it will take us to understand the educational process. Therefore, to ask for a cost-benefit analysis of a specific educational program, where somebody comes up with his C-B number which is supposed to represent the advantage to the nation of having this particular educational program, is ridiculous. It is just coming up with nothing. It is a number but it does not say very much. It does not say anything other than this is a number that the Office of Management and Budget can now take back and decide what they are going to fund next year. And since it is that kind of number, you can hire the consulting firm that will come up with the biggest number. So your only problem is to find the consulting firm that will give you the largest cost-benefit number.

For example, I have been involved in trying to evaluate a new piece of technology, an earth resource satellite that N.A.S.A. sent up a little over a year ago, which takes images of sections of earth's surface every 18 days. Now what is the cost-benefit of this technology? If you look at the studies that have been made, they are ridiculous. What they do is, to say, well, if we knew this much about snowcap, and this much about waterflow, and this much about crops, and so on, we would be able to do thus and so. They never once asked the question whether any manager would do anything about the information if he had it, which of course you need to know to evaluate the technology. The point of my saying is, what is the use of a statement that the benefits of this is X million dollars if the managers use this information, when you know the managers will not use the information? So what we have is a kind of hypothetical, mythological cost-benefit analysis being done on the earth resource satellite, and the figures come out to be 16 billion dollars a year for the United States alone. Mythology is great if you write it correctly, but it has nothing to do with reality. And one of the criticisms of our acceptance of utility theory is that we allowed it to get into such channels as these, into this kind of crass cost-benefit analysis. Of course, there are some good C-B studies, but the great majority of them that I have read, are bunches of nonsense, that are nevertheless apparently being used in federal agencies as a basis for making decisions.

Secondly, as a criticism, there is the notion of social pluralism and the question whether comparisons of human values are possible. This was not a serious problem in the 1950's for management science. It becomes more and more a serious problem as we move into international studies of the sort found in Forrester and the Meadow's book on *Limits to Growth*, where we are trying to take certain notions of utility that are common to us in the more affluent countries and to employ them in the nonaffluent countries. I do not think that this is a serious criticism in the sense that it is a deadly criticism, but it does challenge us as management scientists and possibly economists too, to open up our notions of what utility means in a global sense, and whether the challenge that possible intercultural comparisons are inappropriate is a serious one.

My next criticism (and now I come to really what I think is my crucial criticisms of utility theory) can be illustrated by another story. I have having lunch with John Harsanyi, who is an economist and much interested in sociological theories. We were asked ourselves what we were doing lately and he said, well I am trying to straighten Merton out and get him on a sound functional basis as far as his theory of value is concerned. Then he asked me what I was doing and I said I am much interested in Jung's depth psychology and the theory of values implicit in his work, at which point we smiled at each other and finished the lunch and we have not had another lunch since. There are different attitudes towards this; either you think Jung is a bunch of nonsense or else you really take him very, very seriously and deeply. It is a little hard to find any middle ground in this. You either discard him, or you get into him. I am into him and I find that his theory of depth psychology challenges the traditional notions of utility measurement very, very much. In the initial Freudian version, we began to understand that in depth psychology the simple notion that everybody carries around a kind of unified measure, a utility measure, does not work at all. Each individual is a complex of conflicting values, many of which are unconscious, and of which you are not even aware.

To illustrate, when I was trying to decide whether to go to Berkeley or not I had several other jobs offered. So I used a technique which Ackoff and I borrowed from utility theory which we called "an approximate measure of value." First you put down all the characteristics of the jobs. Then you rank them in terms of the most important and the least important. Then you try applying some utility numbers, which you test by various methods. And then with some probability risk analysis you come up with a value measure for each job. And I did that. The two main offers were from Michigan State University and University of California (Berkeley). I ranked all the characteristics I wanted. I put numbers down, did the whole analysis and the answer was go to Michigan State University, at wich point I tore up the whole analysis and went to Berkeley. What I learned was that I did not know what some of the characteristics were that I had really felt about Berkeley. They were unconscious and were not about to be expressed in any conscious choice on my part.

That much we learned from Freud, that the human individual himself is a complex of conflicting values. I think what Jung added to that, especially in his book called *Psychological Types,* and then in later writings on the archetypes, was that valuation is something much richer than can be attained through the typical thinking process, that the human being is not just a thinking individual, or an information processing individual. In *Psychological Types* it was argued that there are four basic functions: sensation, thinking, intuition and feeling. In the dynamic theory that Jung developed, the four are combined as pairs. Thinking and feeling are functionally somewhat opposites. If you are strong on the thinking function, then probably feeling is an underdeveloped function. If you are strong on sensation, probably intuition is an underdeveloped function. That is interesting, you see, because it says to me that feeling, which is the direct appreciation of what is appropriate, cannot be measured in utility terms.

Subsequently, the writings of Jung and of his followers have indicated all kinds of origins of human values that go deep in the archetypal aspects of the psyche. Greek mythology for example, is just as relevant in considering human values as is any kind of measurement of utility. We have thus begun to understand human values in a much deeper way than we have hitherto been able to do.

Why do I think all this is important for management science? I think it is terribly important for management science because most of our Operations Research projects have never been implemented. That is a modest statement; probably 95% of them have not been implemented.

That is also a modest statement; probably 99% of them have never really been implemented as we intended them to be. We do not understand a great deal about the depth psychology of managers, and the depth psychology of people in general. Until we have a better understanding than is expressed by utility theory, I think our history is going to continue to be the same. Words like "intercommunication," "interaction," and so on, are all very important, but developing a much richer theory of human values than utility theory represents seems to me to be a call for item on the agenda of the future of management science. But I would say, that if economists too do not become interested in these deeper aspects of human values, that depth psychology and similar efforts are trying to understand, then management science will have to pull away from its economic base, and develop a much richer, deeper base of evaluation.

Finally, I should mention morality, which is just a special case, I think, of what I was just talking about. Morality in the classical history of ethics has always been in opposition to utility theory. In the classical Greek times it was the difference in philosophy between the Stoics and Epicureans. The Stoics really believe that we had one thing in life to do and that was to understand nature and reason, and there is no purpose beyond that. Spinoza later on in history repeated the same thing. It is not utility theory that makes up human values for Spinoza, it is understanding. You should not try to justify the existence of understanding by any kind of utility function. You should not justify basic research by pointing out its social utility. You justify basic research because it is a fundamental value, that is all. The same opposition of morality and utility theory occurs between Kant and Bentham who were writing their two famous books about the same time. Kant argued that in addition to Bentham's program of social utility maximization, there is a fundamental law of "morality" that we should follow: never treat other individuals as means only, but as ends withal. Do this, not because it increases our utilities, not because it will make us have fewer crimes, but because it is the driving motive of the moral will.

To summarize, it looks to me as though the value theory that we have been using in management science has been primarily developed by thinking types. If we take Jung's psychology seriously, which I do, then what is called for is a much richer notion of values, to be found I think in philosophical literature, in writers like Heidegger and Kierkegaard, also to be found in literature in novels and poetry, to be found in Hindu philosophy, and many other sources.

Management and problem-solving

E. Johnsen

1. Modelling of managerial problem-solving

In this century we are faced with an enormous development in the theory of problem-solving relating to managerial endeavour. Let the following catchwords illustrate this.

Models of managerial problems	Corresponding economic type of model
Technical problems, running the factory as "a closed machine"	Description of the firm in terms of money and technical units
Scientific management, running the firm more effectively	Marginal reasoning for optimum, claims of rational, economic man
Human relations, the firm should be run in accordance with the goals of the employees	Deviation from rationality and equilibrium seeking
Systems management, the firm is considered an open, dynamic system of men and machines	Total models relating submodels

Status:
The firm is considered as a complex interaction between economic man, psychological man, sociological man, organizational man, technological man, information man, etc.

Status:
The firm is considered as a set of cause-effect relationships; input, transformation and output can be measured in economic and technological terms. The model is a useful reduction of the complex situation in two cases:
1. no feeling of the system,
2. deep personal feeling of the problem caused by scarce resources

The scientific study of management has tried to categorize these disciplines in three relatively well defined (but not mutually exclusive) bodies of theory: the decision theory, the behavioral theory and the systems theory.

If, for a moment, we leave theory for what it is and look at the practitioner, we see that the manager solves his problems as all other people do, including scientists. Let us talk about three broad strategies for problem-solving: the process of analysis (the classical natural sciences methodology), the proces of interaction (interacting with other people in order to solve problems), and the search-learning process, which is partly specific and may partly include the first two.

Contemporary research in management as I would interpret it, is trying to integrate problem-solving strategies and these three broad bodies of theoretical knowledge in order to improve the functioning of the managerial process.

This may be illustrated as in Figure 1.

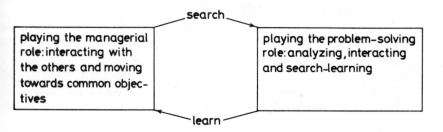

Figure 1. Management and problem-solving.

The interaction between the manager and the management scholar is especially linked to the problem-solving process. As every problem is new and genuine – otherwise it would not be considered a problem – we do not know how to proceed exactly. It depends on the managerial-problem-solving style and it depends on the specific skills of the problem-solving consultant, *i.e.* the scientific role.

Therefore the best one can say is that problem-solving strategies and the disciplines ought to be integrated, *i.e.* all have a chance to be used in the specific problem.

This is illustrated in Figure 2.

Problem-solving strategy   Body of theory (language)

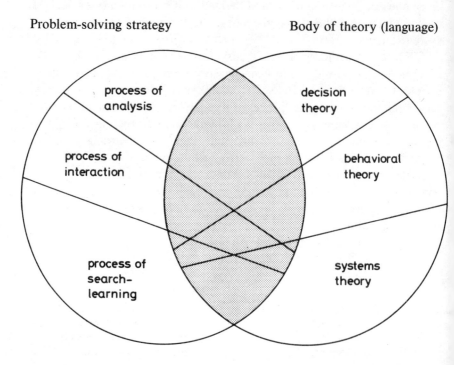

Figure 2. Integration of managerial problem-solving strategy and the disciplines that are relevant for the scientific study of management.

2. Problem-solving strategies in the theory of management

In Figure 3 we have delineated the interaction between the three normal problem-solving strategies and the disciplines relevant to the scientific study of management. The catchwords say something about the actual problem-solving behavior related to the management process. The idea from Figure 2 is that various strategies can, and should, be combined.

The problem-solving strategies seem to be more stable than the disciplines. This will be an argument for the course of our exposition. First we will take the process of analysis and knit it to the problems experienced by managers using this methodology. Next we will take the process of interaction and we will close with the search-learning process.

Relevant Management Disciplines / General Problem-Solving Strategies	Decision Theory	Behavioral Theory	Systems Theory
The Process of Analysis	Goal attainment is an effect of the use of decision-variables in the given situation 1.1.	Behavior in a firm is an interaction between individual, group and organization 1.2	Systems-construction and systems partitioning before systems steering 1.3
The Process of Interaction	Organizing an interaction between the potential partners for total goal attainment due to common means in the given situation 2.1.	Organizing internal "warfare" for an ongoing conflict solution and change of the behavior in the firm / the organization 2.2	Organizing the firm as an internally dynamic and externally open system 2.3
The Search-Learning Process	Information for decision is created through experimentation 3.1.	The behavior in (parts of) the firm is an effect of creative learning 3.2.	The firm is looked upon as a systems process which is coordinated, adaptive, and innovative. 3.3.

Figure 3. The problem-solving strategies in terms of relevant management disciplines.

By the way, this sequence also illustrates the development in the past *25 years of managerial problem-solving endeavour.*

From about 1948 until the middle of the Sixties operations research thinking was developed and absolutely dominating the discussion. OR was in its original form identical to the classical natural science method, here called the process of analysis. Classical OR seems to have come to a crossway. A relative stop in genuine methodological development has been counterweighted by an enormous development in the fields of applications. I think that OR-people for a while will go into search-learning and interaction business and come back with a refined battery of analytical methods.

The process of interaction originated as a genuine strategy in the beginning of the Sixties. The consultant has been aware of the need for different approaches to the problems of the client, the need for different consultation strategies. The client has come to the conviction that the consultant can not solve his problems. The consultant can help him to keep the process going. Therefore the client must help the consultant to help the client to solve his own problems. Process consultation, conflict solution and change consultation are some of the important generators for an ongoing process of interaction. Which by itself seems to be a most important problem-solution strategy in practice. We are still experimenting with interaction strategies and where we are right now is difficult to say.

The search-learning processes have a psychological as well as a cybernetical and computer background. In their newer form they originated in the late Sixties and we are right in the middle of developing this field in such a way that we can talk about a field at all. Pure machine simulation has appeared to be of little use; as a contrast interacting man-machine systems have provided us with many useful insights.

Looking at the top of Figure 3 we see that the relevant management disciplines are synonymous with the languages spoken by practical managers. Comparison with page 102 shows that initially the discussion was being held primarily in the effectiveness language of decision theory. Even that was not invented in its present form.

The behavioral processes – focussed on by theorists in the Thirties – have dominated the discussion in practice in the past twenty years. How do we design our situation such that we can live a normal life in our firms too?

The systems language came up with the computer and ADP and what followed in the information field. Practitioners are working hard to understand systems processes of which they are one part themselves.

Referring to Figure 3, we are faced with a "vertical" development and a "horizontal" development. The result is that we are faced with a development which ties managerial behavior tighter and tighter to scientific management strategies and languages ("models").

This is due to the research strategy of management scholars; we do go into the firms and organizations and work directly on the solution of practical problems *in order to* develop our methodology. On the other hand the practitioner is adapting our languages. This is even easier for him when he is a graduate from one of the scientific management centers.

So practice and theory are amalgamating. Which raises the question as to whether the practitioner has become too theoretical or the theorist too practical. This is a problem in itself and should be treated seriously. We will now proceed to an analysis of the present problems we are facing in the search-learning process between management and problem-solving. The discussion will follow the table in Figure 3, starting with 1.1. and ending with 3.3.

3. Problems in the search-learning process of problem-solving as a tool in the managerial process

Our frame of reference for this discussion is Figure 1 and we will proceed according to Figure 3.

re. 1.1. If you choose to delineate your management problem as a genuine decision problem you must be conscious of your objective(s), decision variables and environmental parameters. You must then work with cause-effect relationships between means and ends until you have created enough information to solve your decision problem.

The management problem is that the more information demanded the less chance that it will be used. The more time you spend at analyzing activities the greater is the chance that the problem "will solve itself". Now and then to the good of the decision maker, now and then to the bad.

re. 1.2. When you try to analyze behavior or a complex behavioral process you model it. In these days we use psychological models of motivation/emotion/cognition types. We use group models of the effectiveness/social-emotional type. We use organizational models of various types. We use political science models focussing on the power/conflict aspect. And we use combinations of these models.

The problem of the manager is that when he uses information from more and more refined behavioral models he gets a more and more specific picture of the behavioral process. Now and then a biased picture. The consequence is: the more analysis the less effect on the behavioral process.

re. 1.3. When a firm/organization is systemized in order to have better steering you have in principle two ways to go. You can build up a new system and/or you can break down an existing system. In any case you get a formalized picture of your system. The experience so far is: the more (and better) systemizing the more pseudosteering and the less systematized behavior.

It is obviously hard for managers to understand that system = information = steering. And it is hard for theorists to acknowledge that this phenomenon is best represented in the managers, i.e. people playing the managerial role.

re. 2.1. If a manager chooses to solve a decision problem by interaction he deliberately chooses a consultant. (He may play the consultant role himself in relation to his fellowmanagers). His problem is that the more help he has from the consultant the less able will he be to make his own decisions, and the less able he will be to influence the ongoing decision process himself.

re. 2.2. Interacting in behavioral terms is very much a matter of "power", "conflict-solution" and "settling things". The philosophy is that we must interact in order to control conflicts. This has always been, so to say, an inborne property of the manager; his personal properties, experience and insight in the situation have made him the normal conflict consultant. Now, his problem is that when you explicitly focus on power and conflict there is a tendency that these aspects become more important in the managerial process and in itself lead to more power issues and create more conflicts.

re. 2.3. Interaction takes time. Communicating with each other and with many others in committees and project groups is time-consuming. If you interact hard in order to coordinate, in order to adapt the system according to environmental changes, in order to influence your environment through innovations, your daily operational activities may suffer.

The managerial problem is to balance the interaction-process over time.

re. 3.1. A search-learning strategy related to a decision problem means experimentation. This causes a lot of problems that are relatively well-known.

The problem of the manager is, however, that the more he experiments with a decision problem the less chance there will be for a proper solution. This is due to the fact that he must experiment "genuinely" with himself, his collegues and the firm. And this is risky.

An ongoing controlled experimentation is a possibility.

re. 3.2. Search-learning in behavioral terms focusses on creative learning. A special environment must be there in order to facilitate creative learning. The managers problem is that this environment is identical with less "steered" behavioral activities. This problem is still to be solved.

re. 3.3. The "best" a manager can do today – according to my experience – is to form a search-learning process as a systems process with an interaction between two elements. That of the process of analysis and that of the process of interaction.

If he succeeds in shaping this *ongoing* process this is identical with coordinating, adaptive and innovative management. The problem of the manager is that he does not believe this.

In *conclusion* it can be said that our present knowledge of how to "help" the management process through experienced types of problem-solving behavior is much greater than 25 years ago. Greater in the meaning of less rigid. We do not have the answer of how to solve a problem. If we had, there existed no problem. But we have the experience that it is necessary to do something. This something being a function of the managerial styles and personalities present, the situation and the norms and traditions of the firm/organization.

A search-learning process between the managerial process and genuine problem-solving is on the one hand a naive and simple "theoretical" claim. On the other hand it is a challenge to the practitioner. And thereby an interesting situation for the interaction between practice and theory in the managerial field. Based on this conclusion we can proceed to the last point.

4. Interaction between the managerial process and the problem-solving process viewed as a search-learning process

Figure 1 has now been elaborated, and we can look at two main consequences of the approach.

One has to do with the development in the styles of management. The other has to do with some moral and ethical issues related to it.

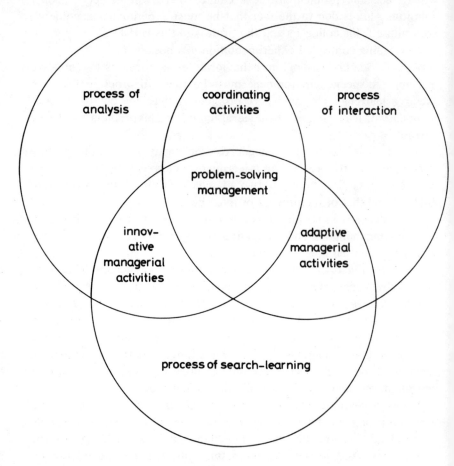

Figure 4. Problem-solving management.

Figure 1 can with the aid of section 3.3. of Figure 3 be reformulated as shown in Figure 4.

Intersection between analysis and interaction means coordinating activities. Intersection between interaction and search-learning means adaptive activities. The intersection between search-learning and analysis means innovative activities.

Figure 4 tells that "Problem-solving management" is the style of today. It consists of a conscious selection of problem-solving strategy (strategies) and a conscious evaluation of one's own management strategy, *i.e.* the way of interacting with the others. This again results in – apart from traditional management styles – three new aspects: coordinating management + adaptive management + innovative management. These should be represented at the same time in the management process.

As it is difficult to have all these three elements represented in the same person we are faced with a group-management style. As a necessity.

This again strengthens the ongoing claim to management of solving its own internal power problems in a "decent" way. A "new" ethics must therefore be developed in order to facilitate this kind of managerial behavior.

Fortunately this kind of ethics will be developed more or less deliberately when the "Probem-solving management" style is performed.

5. Summary

Management is an interaction between you and the others in a goal-directed way. In the managerial process information can properly be created by three common problem-solving strategies: the process of analysis, the process of interaction and the process of search-learning. Communication of results will in practice often appear in terms of decision theory, behavioral theories and systems theory.

These nine combinations of disciplines and problem-solving strategies illustrate partly the present state of knowledge in the steering field and partly the development over the past 25 years. We have faced a change in interest from analytical strategy over interaction strategy to search-learning strategy. And we have faced a change in managerial/problem-solving language from decision problems over behavioral problems to systems problems.

The interaction between managerial behavior and managerial problem-solving behavior can be delineated as a search-learning process. Given our problem-solving knowledge and managerial skill this combination forms the managerial style of today: *problem-solving management*. It is defined with the intersection of coordinative management, adaptive management, innovative management and the three problem-solving strategies.

A consequence of this style is group-based management giving rise to ethical and political problem-solving within the group. This will become a major challenge in the next 10 years.

The value of information

Gordon Wills

Few academic teachers of marketing and logistics would either describe or consider themselves to be economic theorists, although there can be not the slightest room for doubt that marketing knowledge seeks to explain certain facets of economic behaviour in any society. Perhaps the most important reason why marketing and logistics folk do not perceive themselves as economists is simply because they reject the proposition that monetary rationality can on its own offer an adequate explanation of economic activity at the level either of individual customer or firm. Such a statement is not intended to suggest that all economists refuse to countenance any other formative influences on economic behaviour. The overwhelming impression given by theoretical economics is, however, of that ilk.

Whereas an economist may not be unduly taken aback by such a statement, (he may indeed accept it as a realistic reflection of how he intends to be perceived) to a marketing practitioner it is a considerable indictment. Marketing seeks to understand economic activity in order to influence it in a technological or engineering sense, against time and other constraints. It has inevitably been forced to examine the totality of influences at work in shaping any particular act of purchase or company initiative. Whereas an economist can simply regard sociological influences on economic behaviour as something assumed to be constant, in order that he may concentrate the more on economic factors, the marketing man has no such discretions. Rather he must seek out the 'salient' features in the situation, whatever origins they might have. He is accordingly an empiricist first and often a second rate theorist.

Conversely, many economists are first rate theorists working at so remote a level of abstraction and so remote from the realities of the economic activity under examination, that their elegant theories describe and/or predict nothing of real value. Such men also often regard marketing practice as a scurrilous manipulation of quasi divine economic

laws which we are supposed to believe will allocate resources in some
optimum social manner. Marketing is not about selling products which an
entrepreneur has willed to exist. It is the study of how to match
production to the desires and wishes of customers, and of the problems
and issues involved in so doing. How a company can most effectively
share in such a social process is a complex field of study where success
and effectiveness will seldom be the crowns worn by those who worship
simply at the shrines of economic rationality. To take but an instance –
the economics of advertising. Advertising, we are told, shifts the demand
curve. Sometimes, is the truth; but even if we concede the proposition,
we are no wiser about how to advertise. What really matters is where to
advertise, how to advertise and once those decisions are made, how to
measure how well we have done. To perform econometric feats with
sales and promotional expenditure data tells us little if anything at all by
way of explanation of economic activity.

In general, therefore, marketing eschews the grand design. It seeks to
explain through micro-analysis of market situations such small facets of
economic activity as brand switching or purchase source loyalties. As
soon as it does, marketing analysts find themselves looking broadly
across the behavioural sciences for theoretical propositions which might
be of assistance. There is no pride which limits that search for
explanations of economic behaviour; there cannot be since the
consequences of true error or excessive abstraction are often dire in
commercial terms. Such selfdiscipline is seldom visited upon economists
although I gather several monetary economists do have a similar
experience when they advise governments and international institutions.

Marketing's lack of concern with, or will to reform, economic theory,
its unwillingness to wean it away from its dominant mode of approach to
attempting to describe economic activity, is one of the great
disapppointments of the past 25 years. It is scarcely surprising since
marketing has been struggling in many countries to assert itself as a
worthwhile branch of applied economics, as economic engineering,
against the implacable opposition of the power economist. Economics
has also failed at other interfaces such as those with operational research
and with financial management. Such has been the scope of that failure
that today men who wish to understand how the economic world
operates are more likely to study at a business school than in a school of
economics. I do not believe that such a state of affairs is desirable, but I
find that it is virtually inevitable. In general terms, the effective

understanding of, and teaching about micro-economics have shifted away from the theoretical propositions of economics to the synthetic disciplines with their empirical focus. A state of apartheid exists in micro-economics between theory and practice which leads to sterile theory and poorly-learnt lessons of experience. The challenge of the next 25 years must be to destroy the fences which separate us. We must readily admit the truth of the location of micro-economic knowledge – in the management structures and boardrooms of our most successful companies. The true professors and leaders via an understanding of micro-economics will normally be found with the title of Marketing or Finance Director, or Manager. A few of them can be found in business schools. Far too few ever grace the corridors of the economics schools.

Buyer Behaviour as a Focus for Study

Despite these biting criticisms of pure micro-economics, there is a welcome body of knowledge which the brotherhood of economists can claim to have developed over the past score of years which demonstrates the complex nature of the influences at work on a single customer. With the aid of statistics this knowledge can often be aggregated to furnish a valuable set of information and afford an empirical basis for theorising to some effect.

'Buyer behaviour', as the area is dubbed, is a focus for truly multi-disciplinary study. We examine from anthropological and sociological standpoints how we are culturally constrained in our economic activity of buying goods and services; we explore the psychological aspects which influence our decisions; we examine the impact which geographical distance and topography might have; the influence of demography; we identify how technology makes available new modes of consumption behaviour. Marketing's early attempts at integrating these various influences – and more besides – are best demonstrated to date by Amstutz[1] and Howard & Sheth[2] but there are now some five or six treatments in this field and countless papers and sets of readings which adopt this synthesis.

Admittedly, the predominant thrust of these analyses has been in the

1. A. Amstutz (2, 1967).
2. J. Howard and J. Sheth (10, 1971).

area of consumer markets. Yet momentum has been building up very rapidly during the past five years for a closer examination of industrial buying behaviour. It has many similarities with familial decision-making in consumer goods in that the purchaser is often reflecting group pressures and decisions rather than simply his own. (Wind and Webster[3] have perhaps done most in the industrial purchasing area.)

Marketing men examine purchasing behaviour in this total contextual manner because they wish to understand as exactly as possible the dynamics of that behaviour. How, other influences being removed, will the purchaser behave? How can he or she be influenced to behave in any given way that is worthwhile encouraging from the point of view of a specific company, and which is also compatible with the social context in which business is undertaken? The answer which we find is seldom if ever that price taken alone can elicit a required pattern of behaviour. To take but one instance, Gabor and Granger[4], Katona[5], Adam[6] and many more besides have demonstrated quite clearly that there are far more Giffin goods about than that distinguished economist ever imagined. Price is, on more occasions than not, taken as an indicative of quality – and almost always in the absence of branding. Furthermore, assumptions of price knowledge and awareness in a market are likely to be highly misleading. Many of the basic assumptions on which economics has sought to explain buyer behaviour cannot be made if a worthwhile usable theory is to result. The level of abstraction is ludicrous. Usable theories of buyer behaviour are the only category that marketing academics can or will accept. Their students in colleges and in industry demand nothing less.

I realise I am continually discussing the relative degrees of abstraction involved. I have no hesitation as a political economist by training in identifying the marketing academics' approach as considerably more worthwhile simply because it is more likely to give rise to the understanding of fundamental issues which is surely the purpose of all theory construction. The integration of the empirical basis of most marketing analysis of buyer behaviour with the more conventional but intellectually more rigorous approaches of economists must accordingly be one of our major goals over the next 25 years. If marketing scientists

3. F. Webster and Y. Wind (17, 1972).
4. A. Gabor and C.J. Granger (7, 1966).
5. G. Katona (11, 1963).
6. D. Adam (1, 1968).

have been careful to avoid making sweeping assumptions about market conditions, and have overlaid economic theories with a range of more realistic propositions about economic behaviour, they have also conspicuously failed in most cases to develop an adequate theoretical consolidation which can supersede the economist's naive teachings about economic behaviour. For this very reason, a teachable body of marketing knowledge has been shown to emerge and a very considerable emphasis on pragmatism can be seen in its stead. The case method is perhaps the exemplar of pragmatism in management teaching.

Resources Allocation as a Focus

I indicated at the outset that the discipline of marketing can readily be seen as having two predominant foci for analysis. The first, the behaviour of customer, I have now briefly discussed. The second is concerned with the allocation of resources within the operational marketing activity of an enterprise. Economic theory has offered a wide range of analytical approaches, most particularly perhaps the concept of marginalism. The importance of that *concept* is in doubt in terms of profitability analysis; what we know, however, is that it is seldom an effective operational tool. So many factors other than marginal costs (assuming we can and do measure them) affect corporate economic behaviour, *e.g.* brand/market share or product line strategies, critical strategies in promotional activity to gain distribution or defend a position, or social pressures of a national or regional nature, consumerism or environmentalism.

Once more, a total behavioural approach is demanded for the marketing situation if any understanding of an organisation is to emerge. If pricing strategy is to be understood, it must take cognisance of a wide range of non-price factors – such as competitors' wholesale and retail propensity to stock, or the psychological perception of prices by customers, or the level of expectation of after-sales service in market segments. Marginal cost analysis alone within the producing enterprise cannot suffice. It is nowhere near rich enough in its scope.

Now economists can reasonably answer that little of what I have said invalidates the theoretical postulates of marginalism, and by their own terms of reference they can be exonerated. The problem remains that marginalist theory does not explain the behaviour we observe in markets.

Time and time and time again highly knowledgeable and intelligent managers take quite contrary allocation decisions. One of the clearest attempts to explain this behaviour is to be found in Cyert & March's classic work.[7] My colleagues and I have been engaged since 1965 in a wide-ranging series of research studies in marketing which continually identify such patterns of behaviour in relation to individual marketing activities such as test marketing,[8] below-the-line promotion,[9] selection of channels of distribution,[10] selection of overseas markets to penetrate,[11] assessment of advertising effectiveness,[12] the choice of logistics mode,[13] and also in studies of the overall planning of marketing organisation structures.[14] In each and every situation we have examined, economic rationality as an explanation of behaviour had to be rejected because of the intervention of social psychological influences, because of unwillingness to change arising from the social dynamics of proposed change, because of unwillingness to allocate resources to achieve demonstrably economically rational goals. Such consistently deviant behaviour nullifies the validity of economic theories which purport to explain such marketing behaviour. It also nullifies the validity of such propostitions as are contained in a rational economic point of view as catalysts for normative goals towards which we should strive. Surely the reality for management is that most of us strive simply to perform satisfactorily in the organisational context wherein we are employed. Effective and successful management is concerned with trade-offs between competing sets of goals within any enterprise, of which rational economic goals are but one. The best managed and most effective enterprise can be expected to be that which so organises its activities to balance those competing claims.

   The theoretical proposition that the goal of our corporate behaviour is to maximise financial gains is so obviously invalid in most contemporary institutions that I can perhaps turn without further comment to a theoretical prospect which has captivated my imagination for some six years now. The prospect to which I refer is an empirically based assault

7. R.M. Cyert and J.G. March (6, 1963).
8. R. Hayhurst (8, 1968).
9. M.G. Christopher (3, 1972).
10. S.M. Saddik (16, 1971).
11. M. Purnell (15, 1973/74).
12. G.S.C. Wills (19, 1973).
13. M.G. Christopher (4, 1971).
14. R. Hayhurst and G.S.C. Wills (9, 1972).

on the problem of assessing the value of information to an organisation. I hope, through this particular prospect, to demonstrate some of the opportunities which I sincerely believe a judicious combination of marketing empirics and economic rigour can afford.

The Value of Information

My interest in this issue was triggered in 1967 when the UK Market Research Society asked me to cull and edit all the published *Sources of UK Marketing Information* [15] I could into a single volume. I located over 1,000 and in his Foreword, the Chairman of the Society observed that in his view it was unforgivable for any marketing executive to be ignorant of the existence of such information. The publication of the volume, he felt, would do much to fill a very real need to make known the existence of such sources. My immediate and enduring thought was 'how much benefit did all the sweat and tears involved in getting that volume together, bring to its users?'

I was readily able to identify the sales statistics for the book. They were not particularly good, but that I concluded was a separate issue of awareness of the book's existence rather than awareness of existence of the sources listed in the book by any marketing executive, whether or not he had purchased the book. On asking further, however, I found to my consternation that most information services measure their value in sales terms, in terms of the number of people who use their facilities. If enquiries/usage rates/loans go up that is considered indicative of increased value which has been derived from the system. Whilst I would not query the proposition that use is likely to be a *necessary* condition of deriving value from any information system, it can hardly be deemed sufficient. Many titles are misleading, much information has a value which is time-constrained (this is of course especially so for commerce).

In any event, although most systems employ 'usage rates' as a surrogate for value, they implicitly admit by their stocking policies that they do not endorse it. Any public library could readily increase its 'value' by simply stocking multiple copies of all the best-selling novels. Whilst this is normally done up to a particular service level, a point is frequently reached where the information officer concerned will call a

15. G.S.C. Wills (20, 1974).

halt in the interests of 'breadth' of stock. *He will exercise a value judgement which, as I understand it, he is unable to quantify.* I believe that the sort of task we should set ourselves over the next decade or so is finding out how to quantify such values in a generally acceptable manner. I do not know how, any more than social economists yet really know, to assess and aggregate the benefits of arriving home 15 minutes earlier from work. Whilst I do not expect us to be able to produce simple quantified assessments of value, I see no reason why we should not be able to pose an array of alternative choices and perhaps by the use of non-metric scaling methods derive measures of value which can be actionable in management terms.

If such an approach is to be feasible, it will indubitably demand a wealth of empirical evidence to facilitate the formulation of meaningful choices in the face of particular sets of missions open to any enterprise. Indeed, it rapidly becomes apparent that any examination of the value of information can only be commenced in the context of defined missions and then the derived information goals. Yet information systems seldom have meaningfully defined goals against which value can be assessed.

Such thoughts have led my colleagues and I over the past five years to look with considerable care at the obviously tantalising possibility of applying cost/benefit analyses to the problem. We have explored both company test marketing/new product launch decisions[16] and library planning/budgetary models.[17] The economic rationality of Bayesian approaches will be familiar to economists. An expected value of perfect information can be derived using prior probabilities provided by managers, of the occurrence of various outcomes. If we then make realistic assumptions as to how far short of perfect our information will be, *i.e.* we derive conditional probabilities, we can determine via posterior and preposterior analyses whether or not the information improved discriminately in the situation under consideration. Accordingly, we would appear to have a simple decision rule based on economic rationality. Yet despite the fact that all the inputs have been made by a given manager, he will almost invariably refuse to follow the economic logic which emerges. He will refuse to invest on acquiring information, an expenditure equivalent to the benefits which he has indicated will emerge. In many cases, the divergence is vast. Tests and experiments

16. G.S.C. Wills (18, 1970).
17. M.G. Christopher and G.S.C. Wills (5, 1970).

are not done in markets which ought to be done, library budgets are not allocated in directions in which they should be allocated in economically rational terms.

You might wonder why I am dwelling on the economics of information at such length, especially in the context of a 25 year prospect for economic theory. My concern is to emphasise how marketing empirics approach problems and, in particular, how deeply concerned effective marketing is and must be with the quality and availability of information for decision making. Perfect knowledge in any market is a nonsense assumption; imperfection rules, but not only because information cannot be made available to all. Some members of a market-place steadfastly refuse to collect it. They perceive other corporate goals as of greater importance. Equally often, limitations of executive time prevent the quest from being effectively conducted. My plea is for the examination of micro-economics in a framework of corporate politics; it is a plea for the reassertion of the correctness of the study of politics and economics in tandem. Two realistic foci for the next 25 years are, therefore, the political economy of the firm and the political economy of the customer.

Cost/Benefit of Information Services

It may well be useful if I devote the final section of my paper to looking at how the new political economy might relate to the planning of information systems in libraries. The key to success will lie, I believe, in identifying operationally viable methodology whereby the value derived from library services can be meaningfully quantified and compared with the costs incurred in the provision of such services. If we can achieve it in a meaningful managerial sense, guidelines can be developed on the assessment of value and benefit to library users from the services offered, in terms other than sheer quantitative levels of utilization. The reckoning of books issued, of reading desk occupancy and so forth, ignore the value derived from a 'title' of 'seated hour'. Through a continuous dialogue with those who have borrowed books, sat in the library and so forth, we can perhaps seek to identify and then quantify the value or benefit which is being derived from such activities.

Equally, sheer use of a bibliographic system or a card index is no indication of value. Both may prove not to have the information required by the reader. Provision of multiple copies of titles or journals, in order to furnish 95% or 67% service levels (whilst simple enough in operational research terms) is once again not necessarily a measure of the value actually derived.

To attempt to develop a measure of effective value of benefit is a hazardous undertaking. The costing of library services is a similarly difficult task. It is for this reason that I initially propose a modest framework for thought. Let us explore certain limited facets of the library service in order to develop a set of experimental tools for measurement which we can refine and hope to see more widely applied. We have at our disposal the intellectual skills from the areas of attitude scaling, social costing and output budgeting, which are the logical fields of knowledge on which to draw. We can be confident that by taking the value analytic rather than the more directly operational research approach, we can make a unique and considerably overdue contribution. It is a contribution that is indispensible if the discussion of library appropriations, for example, is to advance beyond its present relatively primitive state to a position where some better estimates of the real values derived can be perceived in the context of their costs, and more effective budget allocation made accordingly.

I have conducted an exhaustive review of the background to this strategy to discover what previous attempts have been made to tackle this problem. I regret to report that although there is a considerable amount of writing on output budgeting (PPBS) in library systems, there is very little written on actual installations.

Mrs Maybury covers the problems of programme determination and costing.[18] However, the setting of objectives and evaluation of cost-effectiveness are not examined. Neither does her procedure consider alternative methods and their evaluation.

The "PPBS for Libraries Seminar" (Wayne State University, Spring 1968) produced a number of useful conceptual papers. C. G. Burness discussed "Defining Library Objectives", which covered the full procedure for establishing objectives, together with an extensive list of questions that should be considered. F. Mlynarczyk Jr., in "Measuring Library Costs", considered the problems involved in total system costing. He suggests that conventional business costing procedures be employed. Mlynarczyk, sad to say, relates sales to circulation; inventory to a catalogue department; materials to books and periodicals; and

18. C. Maybury (14, 1961).

production departments to subject classifications, *e.g.* physics or economics.

David Palmer ("Measuring Library Output") pointed to the need for libraries to provide meaningful unit cost information. He perceived a basic need for librarians to know what data required measurement and why. Data sets might then be exposed. His recommendations included:

(i)   statistics should compare the library last year with the library this year, and five years hence;

(ii) the data gathered should be meaningful to the library;

(iii) sampling techniques and experts should be contacted to deal with problems.

The problem of costing information/library services is given a completely different perspective by Harvey Marron, Chief, Educational Resources Information Centre, U.S. Office of Education, ("On Costing Information Services"). He identifies problems peculiar to library installations, *e.g.* :

(i)   a library cannot categorise its output with such precision or certainty as a manufacturing concern;

(ii) information services have special problems in measuring product and service levels;

(iii) depreciation as it is understood in business does not pertain to many information centres. Many assets appreciate. In order to be useful, a document collection must reach a critical size from which it becomes more useful as accessions are made. For reasons of this sort, Marron concludes that business accounting methods are not applicable and directs readers to other contributions by authors looking at the problem from other approaches.

One attempt at measuring cost-effectiveness is suggested by J. E. Martyn in *ASLIB Electronics Group Newsletter,* No. 70, October 1969. Martyn deals with Bulletins produced by specialised information centres which are made up of titles and citations to documents considered relevant to the subject interests of users of the centres. 'Comprehensive effectiveness' is measured by the service coverage of Bulletins with whatever material the user finds from sources outside the service. The method determines relative proportions of interest/non-interest by the user ticking off items of interest to him. 'Currency effectiveness' is compared by checking notification dates with availability dates of material. The objectives he identifies are saving user time, money or effort. To measure whether these are met, a sample of users is asked to indicate items of whose existence they were glad to know. Then, by careful study of the information environment of each sample member, it is suggested that it may be possible to discover the cheapest way each could have found references he marked, had the Bulletin not existed. Ratios may then be produced of Bulletin cost against the national cost for getting the same volume of information by the cheapest alternative means.

King and Lancaster suggest a conceptual framework for a cost/performance/benefit approach to information system evaluation.[19] 'Cost' refers to the input of resources in terms of monetary units. 'Performance' relates to attributes directly controlled by the system, such as recall, precision and speed of response. 'Benefit' is the consequence of system performance in terms of value, ROI, effect on behaviour of the user, direct effect on other systems, and residual non-quantifiable consequences. Flow charts are used to illustrate examples. The problem of cost/effectiveness measurement is not adequately dealt with, however. Lancaster's solo article suggests a number of measurement devices but none are detailed.[20] This paper does, however, suggest potential areas for trade-offs within information systems.

Although there is an extensive literature available and a considerable body of conceptual approaches are proposed therein, few attempts are reported that grapple with the basic problems of determining clear and specific library objectives, costing the services provided to meet them, and assessing the pattern of values derived. It is, therefore, considered that a wider view of cost/benefit be adopted as our starting point. Hence contributions such as E.S. Quade's "Cost-Effectiveness: an Introduction and Overview," and the work of like-minded authors will, we believe, provide the best basis in our search for an apposite methodology and our attempt to implement the output-budgeting approach in library management.

Let us, therefore, take a longitudinal view of the actual and potential use of library services by selected users throughout the full length of a programme of work.

Certain parts of our examination can involve a census of all concerned, but the continuous assessment of derived value from library services can perhaps be undertaken with a sample of those involved. A possible fall-out of up to 20-25% should be allowed for initial samples participating, in order to avoid undermining our purposes. These

19. D.W. King and F.W. Lancaster (12, 1969, pp. 501-505).
20. F.W. Lancaster (13, 1971).

numerical estimates are, however, left open at this juncture for further consideration once the nature of the measurement instruments has been clarified. Any investigation should be conducted in at least four broad stages. They can be separately described in the following terms, although stages II and III will be conducted simultaneously.

Stage I: The identification in specific terms of the objectives for library services to meet the selected needs.

These would be elicited from three groups of informants: leaders, library staff and users. *All* users would be interviewed. One would anticipate that there will be dissonance between the perceived objectives of each group. We should seek to expose and so far as possible reconcile this as a prelude to the further development of our investigation. This reconciled objective or library services mission, is what we can describe as the 'initial normative requirement.'

We should anticipate that perceptions of the actual requirement of library services will change as time progresses, most particularly in the view of the users concerned. We should seek to measure this movement in perception at intervals throughout, continuing to interview all users concerned. The contrasting opinions of those who do, and those who do not, make extensive use of library services will be noted in particular.

We could perhaps commence work on Stage I from the basis provided by C.G. Burness, as described earlier.

Stage II: The identification in specific terms of the costs implicit in providing the levels of library service deemed to meet the initial normative requirement.

This part of the investigation, which will involve library staff in particular, will examine all costs attributable to mission fulfilment in PPBS terms. Where economies of scale accrue they will be identified and notional allocations made at both discrete and actual operational levels, and their implications explored.

It will be appreciated that the PPBS approach cuts across conventional budgeting lines which normally allocate costs to accessions, issues, *etcetera*. In identifying the most appropriate approach to employ, we can take as our starting point the contrasting views of Mlynarczyk and Marron, as described earlier.

Stage III: The identification, on an on-going basis throughout the courses selected, of the perceived value of each library service received and the perceived loss of value for each library service not received when required.

The development of specific research instruments here presents perhaps the major challenge. We should attempt to assess each library service deployed in scale terms on at least two dimensions: relative value to the whole span of services provided, and specific value for the need at hand. Though the continuous compilation of weekly diaries by all sample members, supplemented by three/four personal interviews during the time period, as well as formal briefing and debriefing sessions at the commencement and end of the period, general data can be elicited.

Such detailed scrutiny of the use of library services is almost certain to influence the 'typicality' of any sample. To gain some insight into the nature of such biases, non-sample members of the groups concerned should be consulted on occasion to assess their reactions to certain situations also experienced by sample members.

Stage IV: The reconciliation of cost and benefit data to improve the management of library resources.

From the data derived in Stages I and III we shall have obtained an overall perspective on the normative requirement and the relative values placed on specific services available at various points in time. We should also have, from Stage II, a reasonably clear impression of how costs have been incurred in providing services. The matching of these two sets of data to compare the reported benefits against costs – when reconciled with maximum cost constraints – should indicate to what extent the pattern of services can be modified.

It is such a process of reconciliation which examples economic engineering, or marketing technology. We have described how user information can be collected as a basis for understanding behaviour and of then acting to affect or improve the circumstances. At the risk of excessive repetition, it is in foci such as these that marketing empirics and economic theoretical rigour can come together. I believe that they soon will.

Summary

Marketing practitioners found very little of immediate value in economic theory when they began to develop their own body of knowledge in the fifties and sixties. The attempt to explain behaviour solely in terms of economic man, and the levels of abstraction adopted, meant that marketing had to develop its own range of basic propositions. Without the benefit of an intellectually rigorous tradition, however, marketing's contribution has been predominantly piecemeal. Economics, for its part, has tended to scorn the empirically based pragmatism of marketing, failing often to recognise that it constitutes a rich source for developing a viable, useful theory of economic behaviour albeit without exclusive reliance on economic rationality.

The paramount lesson to be learnt from marketing at this juncture is that economic behaviour can normally only be explained in multi-disciplinary terms. The paper takes this lesson and explores its meaning in terms of the behaviour of buyers and of operational marketing executives.

By way of a prospect on the next 25 years, a critique of economic rationality in the field of information buying is developed and a framework for a multi-disciplinary approach suggested. The problem of valuing information in multi-disciplinary terms is explored. The imperfect quality of the information used in micro-economics decision making, and the lack of enthusiasm on the part of executives to buy on economically, rational terms are, it is suggested, fundamentally important phenomena to understand if organizational goals − be they simple economic, behavioural or a combination of both − are to be attained. Intellectual rigour is required in the face of such problems which a synthesis of the traditions of economic theory and empirical pragmatism of marketing can provide; the challenge to let this happen lies before us over the next 25 years.

References

1. Adam, D., *Les reactions du consommateur devant le prix*, Paris, 1968.
2. Amstutz, A., *Computer Simulation of Competitive Market Response*, 1967.
3. Christopher, M.G., *Marketing Below-the-line*, 1972.
4. Christopher, M.G., *Total Distribution*, 1971.

5. Christopher, M.G. and G.S.C. Wills, "Cost Benefit of External Information," *UNESCO Library Bulletin,* January, 1970.
6. Cyert, R.M. and J.G. March, *A Behavioral Theory of the Firm,* 1963.
7. Gabor, A. and C.J. Granger, "Price as an Indication of Quality," *Economica*, 1966.
8. Hayhurst, R., *Test Marketing in Practice,* BIM, 74, 1968.
9. Hayhurst, R. and G.S.C. Wills, *Organizational Design for Marketing Futures,* 1972.
10. Howard, J. and J. Sheth, *Theory of Buyer Behavior,* 1971.
11. Katona, G., *Psychological Analysis of Economic Behavior,* 1963.
12. King, D.W. and F.W. Lancaster, "Cost Performance and Benefits of Information Systems," *Proceedings of the 32nd Annual Meeting of the American Society for Information Science,* VI (1969), pp. 501-505.
13. Lancaster, F.W., "The Cost/Effectiveness Analysis of Information Retrieval and Dissemination Systems," *Journal of the American Society for Information Science,* January-February, 1971.
14. Maybury, C., "Performance Budgetting for the Library," *ALA Bulletin,* January, 1961.
15. Purnell, M., *Identifying European Marketing Opportunities,* Cranfield Research Papers in Marketing and Logistics, 1973/74 session.
16. Saddik, S.M., "Manufacturer Toleration of Channels of Distribution," Ch. 7 in G.S.C. Wills, *Exploration in Marketing Thought,* 1971.
17. Webster, F. and Y. Wind, *Organization Buying Behaviour,* 1972.
18. Wills, G.S.C., "Cost Benefit of a Test Market," in G.S.C. Wills and J. Seibert (eds.), *Marketing Research,* 1970.
19. Wills, G.S.C., "Pragmatism in Advertising Research," *Journal of Advertising,* 1973.
20. Wills, G.S.C., *Sources of UK Marketing Information,* 2nd edition, 1974.

Final observations

A. Bosman

In the last 25 years economics as a science has been influenced by a number of developments. I will just mention three of these developments. The first is the *computer* with its logical result in the form of computer science and electronic data processing. The second is *marketing*. Economics, especially managerial economics, was mainly directed toward problems in finance, organization theory, cost accounting and production planning. The third is the development and the resulting *impact on economics of the social sciences,* especially psychology and sociology. To make things more complicated: the developments I mentioned are interrelated. To give just one example: developments in cognitive psychology are connected with those in computer science, for instance, on the subject of artificial intelligence. One of our distinguished lecturers, Professor Simon, did quite a lot of research in this field.

During the lectures of the last three days on the scientific research into management, our guests paid attention to two of the three developments mentioned. Professors Simon and Churchman talked about the impact of the social sciences; Professor Johnsen talked about the impact of the social sciences in organizations and Professor Wills discussed the influence of marketing, especially marketing as it relates to organizations. I can imagine that a number of you, especially those who finished their studies more than ten years ago, had difficulties in connecting the main ideas of the four lectures. The purpose of my attempt at summarizing them is to define at least one connection. For that purpose I will make use of some features of scientific method.

Let us start with the lecture of Professor Churchman. I think that the main point of his lecture is his idea to extend what he called the value base – the value system. One can connect a value system with the idea Professor Simon was talking about, and what I will call a *procedural system.* Professor Johnsen went one step further and defined a procedural system within an organizational system. And then going into even more detail, Professor Wills talked about one subsystem of the organizational system – the marketing system.

The connection between the four lectures is shown in figure 1. This connection is one of specialization. The big problem, however, is how to define the arrows in figure 1. The first arrow is probably the most difficult to define. In his lecture and during the discussion Churchman was rather vague about its content. Churchman stated that the set of variables in the value system is much broader than the subsystem of economic variables we generally use. When you have to make the value sets wider, a number of problems appear and I will just mention two.

Figure 1

The first problem is the measurement of values. How do you measure these new variables? Professor Wills made a few remarks regarding this problem and from these remarks it is quite clear that already at this instance we meet a number of methodological difficulties. The second problem is even more difficult because there is a very large probability that the objective function to be defined is not a linear one and that the variables in it are not independent. It is my opinion, that it is impossible to find a satisfactory solution for these methodological problems, at least at this moment. So we have to look for other solutions and Churchman made two suggestions, I believe, in that direction.

The first one is *to use constraints*. By using additional constraints in mathematical or linear programming, it is possible to take into consideration a number of aspects and to evaluate them indirectly with the help of shadow prices. In this respect, let me remind you of a statement made by Simon a few years ago in which he says "if I may specify the constraints everybody else may specify the objective function." The specification of the constraints is in most cases much more important than the specification of the objective function. That is one possibility of finding a solution. The other possibility Churchman mentioned is *teleological rationality*. In teleological rationality we take the goals as given, we try to construct procedures in order to find an optimal or a good solution. And let me remind you, teleological rationality is not a set of techniques that delivers *the* solution, but a set that will give you *a* solution. Just the difference between "the" and "a" opens possibilities for using teleological rationality as an instrument for extending the value base.

With the help of teleological rationality we can reach the concept of a procedural system. The notions teleological rationality and procedural system are not identical but they overlap to a large extent. In a procedural system we may try to construct procedures which specify the way people act or should act. If you try to specify the latter, stressing the point how they should act, we are normative in the way we generally use that term in economics. Procedures deal with the decisions people or groups of people make. In management we are especially interested in the way people make decisions in organizations. I define *organization* as a set of decision procedures of individuals and groups of individuals in relation to certain goals and dealing with the allocation of scarce means of production necessary to reach these goals. This is a rather broad definition of an organization which opens, by the way, the possibility of referring to the social sciences, as we are starting from individuals and groups of individuals.

Professor Simon discussed the procedural systems, especially with reference to one of the main techniques we use to give substance to these procedures, namely *planning*. Planning is the most important set of techniques we have to deal with when using these procedures in a normative context. There are other techniques, but they are less important and I will ignore them. Professor Johnsen showed us one way,

I think, to define a procedural system in an organization. In our department we are doing research in another way.

In our department we pay special attention to the aspect of data processing and a manner to specify the relations between procedures. The latter aspect is important because when you are dealing with the relations between elements it is possible to use system theory. System theory is a body of knowledge which could be quite useful when trying to find solutions for organizational problems. If we define an organization as an open system, and Professor Wills, last but not least, touched upon this aspect, we must conclude that marketing is not the only function – set of procedures – that is dealing with the environment, although it certainly is *the* function that is performing that task. As the relations with the environment have all the features of being ill-structured, a procedural system has all the possibilities to start its life in marketing.

The central question that is relevant for the idea and the construction of procedural systems is the validity of the representation of a problem. If you take that point of view, two things are happening. One way already mentioned by Churchman when he said that we are not talking about management sciences but about sciences in management. We are inclined not to look at just one way, or one procedure to specify the environment, but we are trying to get a grip on every procedure that opens a possibility to improve the representation. Whether these procedures come from psychology or from system engineering or from computer science does not matter. This is quite a different approach from the general one in which a distinction between sciences is made according to a subject matter. That is one point; the second is that stressing the relevance of the representation leads to different strategies in solving problems. Whether these problems are economic problems or problems with an economic aspect is again the central question.

I will show you with the help of the idea of the so-called modelcycle three different ways to solve the problem of model building and also the problems of representation.

The first modelcycle will be called the *axiomatic modelcycle,* see figure 2. It is widely used in economics, especially in *general* economics. This modelcycle starts with observations. That is a remarkable start, because one cannot assume that a research process is started as a random procedure as far as observations are concerned. As the start of every modelcycle is rather vague, I assume that in the second box of this modelcycle preliminary relations are defined. In the next step

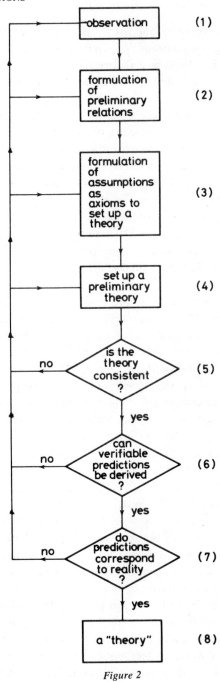

Figure 2

assumptions in the form of axioms are introduced to set up a preliminary theory. There are two means of control to check whether this preliminary theory can become a theory.

a. A check on consistency and efficiency of which the former is the most important.
b. A check meant to investigate whether verifiable predictions can be derived and whether these predictions do correspond to reality.

With regard to the representation problem one can conclude that the inductive aspects of the problem formulation in the axiomatic modelcycle are very weak. There are two main reasons which are responsible for this fact.

1. The axioms are generally of an ideal-type construction, in the sense in which Max Weber used that notion. These types of constructions are not in correspondence with reality, so it is correct if they are used as axioms. Axioms cannot, however, be validated directly. So the box in which the question is stated whether verifiable predictions can be derived can only be answered in the affirmative if one realizes that the questions asked must be of a very general nature, for instance questions about the nature of the signs and the magnitude of the parameters in the model.

2. In order to check whether these "predictions" correspond with reality we must derive data that describe reality. Reality is not, by definition, an ideal-type situation. So if the "predictions" are accepted we can only conclude that the axioms are specifying a situation that is in accordance with reality. We do not have any guarantee that this specification is the best possible nor do we have a guarantee that the procedure for the estimation of the parameters delivers an outcome that is a valid one as seen from a point of view of making predictions from a point of view of representation of the past. The axiomatic modelcycle does not offer any specification of the way reality must be described.

For the purpose of given directives on how to estimate relationships and parameters in a model we can use the second modelcycle. This modelcycle is called the *econometric* modelcycle, see figure 3. There are a number of differences between the first and the second modelcycle. I will mention two important ones.

1. The second modelcycle pays more attention to the process of induction. The predictions are made on the basis of estimations of parameters and relationships representing reality. So in the sphere of representation a number of techniques are presented that make it possible to describe reality in a consistent and efficient way. The hard

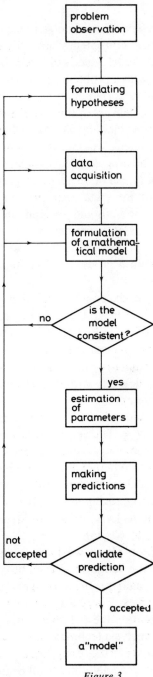

Figure 3

core of econometrics is the specification of techniques according to a number of criteria dealing with consistency and efficiency.

2. The start of the second modelcycle is different from the one in the first modelcycle. One starts with a problem observation and formulation of hypotheses. For the problem formulation econometrics is, at least in most cases, specifying the problem according to a theory that is delivered with the help of the axiomatic modelcycle. So, what the econometric modelcycle really does is to check whether the axioms of modelcycle 1 are not rejected by reality. The process of formulating the axioms, or the making of a depiction of reality, is not an accepted part of econometrics. Of course it is possible to integrate that part in the econometric modelcycle. In that case one should extend the formulation of hypotheses to a process that is also directed by the information of the feedback of not accepting the prediction. In that case, however, it will in general be difficult to maintain a process of hypothesis formulation of axioms of the ideal-type kind.

Taking up the last suggestion, the conclusion is that if one wants to pay more attention to the process of making a valid depiction of reality one has to stress the importance of the induction phase of the modelcycle. In the third modelcycle I will give an example as to how this can be done. This modelcycle is called the *inductive orientated modelcycle,* see figure 4.

If we compare the third modelcycle with the other two it appears that there are three important differences.

a. The formulation of the problem demands a specification of a relation as sketched in box (2) of figure 4. The set of exogenous variables is not restricted to the so-called economic variables. Every variable that could have an influence is accepted. Whether these variables are studied by psychology or by any other science is irrelevant.

b. In the induction phase each exogenous variable is separately tested with the endogenous variable to look for a dependency between both. This is the loop from box (2) to box (5).

c. As a result of the induction phase we have a set of k exogenous variables, in general $k < n$. In the deductive phase, box (7) and box (8), a model is constructed. The main problem is specifying the relations between the exogenous variables. There are different ways in which to find these relations. I will mention the two main ones.

1. The use of multivariate analysis techniques. As I assume, however, that there are relations between the exogenous variables, one will encounter different problems, especially multicollinearity.

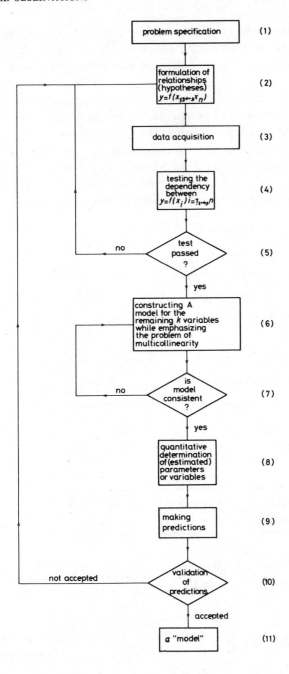

Figure 4

2. The use of simulation as a method of research. In that case, we will generally assume certain relationships between the exogenous variables and check whether certain sets of these relationships correspond with reality.

With these three modelcycles I have tried to give you an impression of the development of economics as a science and to relate the lectures of our four guests to this development. Our guests were dealing with problems of implementing procedures in order to obtain better descriptions of reality. All four were trying to tackle the problems of making a depiction of reality without using axioms as a start for the construction of a model. Instead, procedures play an important role

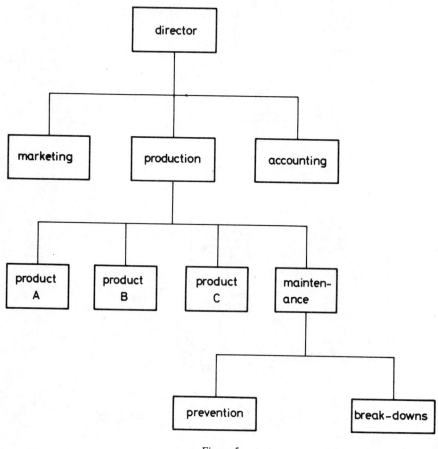

Figure 5

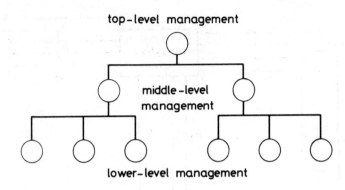

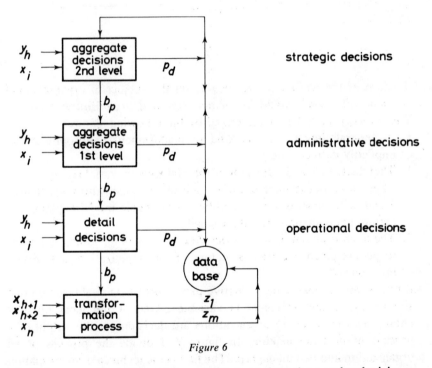

Figure 6

when it comes to defining how people act when they make decisions. Before ending my attempt to summarize I will give an example of the differences between the three modelcycles when trying to apply them in the field of organizational problems.

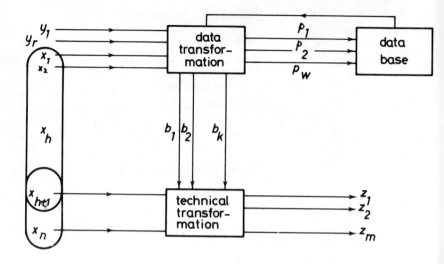

Figure 7

If one uses the axiomatic modelcycle on the subject of organizational problems the result could be named *classical organization theories.* These theories can be characterized by the following features.

1. In general they use some kind of management philosophy as an implicitly defined axiom.
2. They lack a clear description of the endogenous variables.
3. They make an extended use of models of an iconic nature, see figures 5 and 6. In general the possibilities of an iconic model explaining a certain phenomenon are rather small.
4. The main problem these theories deal with, is of allocating functions to people given a certain structure of the organization and certain procedures.

If one wants to enlarge the inductive part of organizational research one should try to find endogenous variables. One of the most obvious endogenous variables in organizations are decisions as the output of a process of decision making. In figure 7, I divide the process of an organization into two main parts. The first is the technical transformation part described by equation (1). In economics equation (1) is called the production function. The second is the decision part described by equation (2). The decision part as a transformation process could be presented as a process of data transformation. For the explanation of the

x_g = input resources
x_i = input resources for start of the production process
z_j = final products
y_h = external data
p_d = internal data
b_p = decisions

$$z_j = f(x_i) \tag{1}$$
$$b_p = g(x_g, y_h, p_d) \tag{2}$$

$g = 1,2,........, h, ..., n$
$i = h+1, ..., n$
$j = 1,2, ..., m$
$h = 1,2, ..., r$
$d = 1,2, ..., w$
$p = 1,2, ..., k$

process of allocating scare means of production the information in (1) is less relevant than the information produced by (2). Equation (1) is specifying a number of alternatives, equations as (2) define the decision process. The specification as described by (2) is, without any doubt, too general. I will just mention two ways that can be used to give a contents to the description of (2). The first is by using the econometric modelcycle. In that case we generally define a system of simultaneous equations. In that system it is possible to connect the relevant endogenous variables. The second is what I call the aggregated simulation approach, which uses the inductively oriented modelcycle as a guide for research. An example of such an approach can be found in the work of J.W. Forrester.

The problem of finding a good depiction of the decision process in organizations is the central objective of organizational research in the last decade and it will probably be so in the near future. The four lectures given dealt with that problem.

I hope, I have given you with the help of some aspects of scientific method a view of the different ways we can obtain better representations of the problems in organizations. Let us hope that this opens the possibility of finding better solutions for these problems too.

Appendix

The organization of this conference was made possible by financial support of the following companies.

Aagrunol B.V., Groningen

Aannemersbedrijf N.J. Evenhuis, Hoogkerk

Aannemings- en Wegenbouwbedrijf
P.H. Offringa B.V., 't Harde

Aluminium Delfzijl N.V., Delfzijl

Atlanta, Hoogezand B.V., Hoogezand

Ballast-Nedam Groep N.V., Amsterdam

Billiton International Metals B.V., 's-Gravenhage

B.V. Aannemers- en Wegenbouwbedrijf
Sjouke Dijkstra en Zoon, Aduard

Coöp. Aan- en Verkoopvereniging
"Aankoop Centrale Groningen G.A.," Groningen

Coöp. Melkproduktenbedrijven
Domo-Bedum G.A., Beilen

Coöp. Melkproduktenfabriek
"De Ommelanden," Groningen

Corning Nederlandse Fabrieken B.V., Groningen

Danlon Hin N.V., Emmen

Elektronics Holland N.V.,
Accounting Dep., Heerenveen

Feenstra Verwarming N.V., Heerenveen

Hollandsche Beton Maatschappij B.V., Amsterdam

Hoofdkantoor "C &1 A" Nederland, Amsterdam

Hoogovens IJmuiden B.V., IJmuiden

Keip B.V., Groningen

Klynveld, Kraayenhof en Co.
Accountants, Amsterdam

Nederlandsche Aanneming Maatschappij
Nedam B.V., 's-Gravenhage

Nederlandsche Accountants-Maatschap, Rotterdam

N.V. Carton fabriek
Beukema en Co., Hoogezand

N.V. Raadgevend Efficiency Bureau
Bosboom en Hegener, Amsterdam

N.V. Uitgeversmij Elsevier, Amsterdam

Mous N.V., Bakhuizen

Opti-Nederland, Winschoten

Philips N.V., Eindhoven

Rottinghuis Aannemingsbedrijf, Groningen

Sluis-Machinefabrieken N.V., Drachten

Staalmeubel N.V., Roden

Tapijtfabriek H. Desseaux N.V., Oss

Thomassen en Drijver, Deventer

Trelleborg Rubberfabrieken N.V., Hoogezand